─── PRAISE

THE LIFE-GIVING CHURCH

A gold mine of successful ideas born out of practical experience!
The Life-Giving Church is must reading for anyone who wants to
be part of a thriving, growing church.

DR. DON ARGUE
PRESIDENT, NORTHWEST COLLEGE
SEATTLE, WASHINGTON

Ted Haggard is one of the most life-giving guys I have ever met!
His teachings and insights have been a great inspiration and help to
our leadership team. *The Life-Giving Church* is a must read for
growing churches, their laypeople and their pastors.

JOHN ARNOTT
SENIOR PASTOR, TORONTO AIRPORT CHRISTIAN FELLOWSHIP
TORONTO, ONTARIO

A man of prayer and a true pastor with a shepherd's heart,
Ted Haggard has learned how to combine the spiritual and the
practical in his life and ministry. I recommend this book with
enthusiasm to anyone seeking to learn more about Christ-centered
ministry that releases the vibrant life of the Holy Spirit.

MIKE BICKLE
PASTOR, METRO CHRISTIAN FELLOWSHIP
KANSAS CITY, MISSOURI

Godly wisdom flows from *The Life-Giving Church* like fresh, cool water upon dry, parched land. I believe God will use this book to bring refreshing new life, His life, to many thousands of churches, pastors and Christian organizations.

BILL BRIGHT
FOUNDER AND PRESIDENT, CAMPUS CRUSADE FOR CHRIST
ORLANDO, FLORIDA

The powerful substance of this book flows from the simplicity of its message, translated from Scripture into understanding, admonition and inspiration for daily life and ministry. *The Life-Giving Church* is a must for all in the Body of Christ seeking empowerment and direction for their homes, lives and ministry!

DR. LUIS BUSH
INTERNATIONAL DIRECTOR, A.D. 2000 & BEYOND MOVEMENT
COLORADO SPRINGS, COLORADO

The central message of *The Life-Giving Church* is that churches should be avenues of life, not death. Ted Haggard dispenses life and offers practical insights for churches desiring to do the same.

CLIFFORD R. CHRISTENSEN
CONFERENCE MINISTER, CONSERVATIVE CONGREGATIONAL CHRISTIAN CONFERENCE
ST. PAUL, MINNESOTA

Ted Haggard offers the Church a unique opportunity: a behind-the-scenes look at one of America's model churches. The journey is amazingly candid, transparent and honest, without hype or empty promises. It is a journey of God's grace flowing through a yielded congregation. There is a tangible hope in these pages for every church to become a life-giving church for its city, its region and for the nations.

FRANK DAMAZIO
SENIOR PASTOR, CITY BIBLE CHURCH
PORTLAND, OREGON

The Life-Giving Church is refreshing and empowering. The Body of
Christ *needs* this book to experience a bold new way of life.

KINGSLEY FLETCHER
PASTOR, LIFE COMMUNITY CHURCH
RESEARCH TRIANGLE PARK, NORTH CAROLINA

Before the Lord released the harvest at Pentecost, He prepared
and empowered His apostles. Today, the Lord again is preparing leaders
with a view toward the great multitudes that will soon come to Him.
With wisdom, passion and joy, Ted Haggard reveals the heart we must
have if we are to gather souls on the day of harvest.
The Life-Giving Church is an invaluable resource.

FRANCIS FRANGIPANE
SENIOR MINISTER, RIVER OF LIFE MINISTRIES
CEDAR RAPIDS, IOWA

Ted Haggard has walked each step of the life-giving principles he imparts,
and we see his footprints clearly as they follow the Life Giver.

JANE HANSEN
PRESIDENT, AGLOW INTERNATIONAL
EDMONDS, WASHINGTON

Ted Haggard's warmth of heart and his genuine, love-motivated zeal
for the ministry of Christ's kingdom flavor everything he does.
Wisdom and life flow as he shares, because he maintains a humble
heart toward God and an intimate walk with Jesus.

JACK W. HAYFORD
FOUNDING PASTOR, THE CHURCH ON THE WAY
VAN NUYS, CALIFORNIA

The Life-Giving Church is not only a book for pastors but for any member of a local church. It answers many of the questions concerning what goes on with the leadership of the church. Ted Haggard's writing style is refreshing, open and honest. This book will be a great blessing to all in the Body of Christ.

CINDY JACOBS
COFOUNDER, GENERALS OF INTERCESSION
COLORADO SPRINGS, COLORADO

The Life-Giving Church is a must read for all levels of leadership in the local church. Ted Haggard lays out the practical and simple principles that are essential (yet often lacking) for building a healthy local church. This book will make you take spiritual inventory of your church— and a hard look at your own heart and motives—while giving you new insight and hope for your future.

JOHN P. KELLY
EXECUTIVE DIRECTOR, INTERNATIONAL COALITION OF APOSTLES
SOUTHLAKE, TEXAS

Ted Haggard's contagious smile and fervent energy for life-giving ministry is written on every page of this book. With the heart of a servant, he inspires us all to give our Spirit-filled lives to the Kingdom work of the Church.

STEPHEN A. MACCHIA
PRESIDENT, VISION NEW ENGLAND
BURLINGTON, MASSACHUSETTS

Delightful and filled with practical application and wisdom! Every pastor should encourage his flock to read *The Life-Giving Church*. It is wonderful to find a book that will assist the Church in establishing spiritual boundaries while at the same time causing spiritual life and victory to abound.

CHUCK D. PIERCE
DIRECTOR, GLORY OF ZION MINISTRIES
COLORADO SPRINGS, COLORADO

The Life-Giving Church is a must read for every pastor! Ted Haggard provides a smorgasbord of progressive ideas that, when implemented, will transform the way we do church. The message is timely and desperately needed. I highly recommend it!

DUTCH SHEETS
SENIOR PASTOR, SPRINGS HARVEST FELLOWSHIP
COLORADO SPRINGS, COLORADO

THE
LIFE
Giving
CHURCH

TED HAGGARD

Regal

A Division of Gospel Light
Ventura, California, U.S.A.

Published by Regal Books
A Division of Gospel Light
Ventura, California, U.S.A.
Printed in the U.S.A.

Regal Books is a ministry of Gospel Light, an evangelical Christian publisher dedicated to serving the local church. We believe God's vision for Gospel Light is to provide church leaders with biblical, user-friendly materials that will help them evangelize, disciple and minister to children, youth and families.

It is our prayer that this Regal book will help you discover biblical truth for your own life and help you meet the needs of others. May God richly bless you.

For a free catalog of resources from Regal Books/Gospel Light, please call your Christian supplier or contact us at 1-800-4-GOSPEL *or* www.regalbooks.com.

Cover and Interior Design by Robert Williams
Revised edition edited by Deena Davis

Library of Congress Cataloging-in-Publication Data
Haggard, Ted.
        The life-giving church / Ted Haggard.—Rev. ed.
            p. cm.
        ISBN 0-8307-2659-4 (trade paper)
Church management. I. Title.

BV652 .H26 2001
253—dc21   2001016095

2 3 4 5 6 7 8 9 10 11 12 13 14 15 / 09 08 07 06 05 04 03 02 01

Rights for publishing this book in other languages are contracted by Gospel Literature International (GLINT). GLINT also provides technical help for the adaptation, translation and publishing of Bible study resources and books in scores of languages worldwide. For further information, contact GLINT, P.O. Box 4060, Ontario, CA 91761-1003, U.S.A. You may also send e-mail to Glintint@aol.com, or visit their website at www.glint.org.

DEDICATION

In 1971, Pastor Jon Gilbert was sent by the Home Mission Board of the Southern Baptist Convention to Yorktown, Indiana, to plant a church. While the church was temporarily meeting in the American Legion hall, some of my high school buddies invited me to visit. That visit resulted in a group of us driving with Pastor Jon to Explo '72 in Dallas, Texas, where I accepted Christ as my Savior.

As I continued in high school, my Christian life was shallow and lacked commitment. Then, just after I graduated from high school, I was enjoying an exciting weekend night with my friends when my life was suddenly changed.

It was the summer of 1974, and by this time, Jeff Floyd had come to pastor Yorktown Baptist Church. The church had recently built a new building, and Pastor Jeff was temporarily living in a trailer nearby until a parsonage was prepared. My buddies and I knew that he was alone in the trailer; so late one night we drove our cars in circles around his trailer until we saw a light come on. Then we drove off only to return in another hour when we were sure the pastor had gone back to bed. After three or four episodes of this mischievous behavior, we unexpectedly saw Pastor Jeff standing in the glow of our headlights. Our cars screeched to a stop. Much to our chagrin, Jeff invited us in. With a gentle spirit and a well-worn Bible, he brought us to our knees on his living room floor. God touched us that night and our lives were forever changed.

Jon Gilbert and Jeff Floyd will probably never be on the cover of *Charisma, Christianity Today* or *Ministries Today* magazines, although I think it would be great if they were. And I doubt that either of them will aspire to write a book that hundreds of thousands will read—although I think we would all benefit if they did. Nor will either of them pastor a megachurch and enjoy its attendant benefits. But they and thousands of pastors like them will pray for us, silently sit with us while we cry, perform our weddings and funerals, answer the phone when we call and faithfully care for our families as well as their own. They will drive vans loaded with our kids to Christian events and bless us in countless other ways.

I think these pastors are heroes. It is because of them that more Americans attend church services every Sunday than attend all of our major sporting events for an entire year combined. As time passes, these pastors accumulate thousands of believers, in myriad churches, who are living healthy lives because of their godly example of teaching and loving us. Often we don't even acknowledge them with a warm thank-you.

It is to these pastors we dedicate this book. Jon and Jeff are symbols of the thousands of faithful pastors who come when they are called, sacrifice all for the cause of Christ and unyieldingly serve His kingdom.

Thank you, Jon Gilbert. Thank you, Jeff Floyd. We all thank you very much.

CONTENTS

FOREWORD

Back in 1985, a young pastor serving on the staff of Bethany World Prayer Center of Baker, Louisiana, which now numbers upwards of 8,000, sensed a clear call from the Lord to launch out and plant a new church in Colorado Springs. With the agreement, the support and the covering of his senior pastor, Larry Stockstill, Ted Haggard moved his family to Colorado Springs and began New Life Church. Colorado Springs was not then the center of evangelical Christianity that it is today, but 1985 is widely regarded as the year that things in the city began to change for the good. One indication of the influence that New Life Church now has in Colorado Springs is the fact that some 6,000 believers show up for worship every Sunday.

When Ted Haggard first arrived in Colorado Springs, then a New Age center that was economically and socially depressed, he had no district superintendent or home mission board to direct his activities and to give him a tried-and-true strategy for planting a new church. Rather than serving under a traditional denomination, Ted represented a new form of carrying out the life and ministry of the Church, which I have been calling the New Apostolic Reformation.

WHAT IS THE NEW APOSTOLIC REFORMATION?

The New Apostolic Reformation is an extraordinary work of God that began at the close of the twentieth century and continues on. It is, to a significant extent, changing the shape of Protestant Christianity around the world. For almost 500 years, Christian churches have largely functioned within traditional denominational structures of one kind or another. Particularly in the 1990s, but with roots going back for almost a century, new forms and operational procedures are now emerging in areas such as local church government, interchurch relationships, financing, evangelism, missions, prayer, leadership selection and training, the role of supernatural power, worship and other important aspects of church life. Some of these changes are being seen within denominations themselves, but for the most part they are taking the form of loosely structured apostolic networks. In virtually every region of the world, these new apostolic churches constitute the fastest-growing segment of Christianity.

Church planting is built right into the very fabric of new apostolic leaders. Nothing could be more predictable than being on the staff of a new apostolic church in our nation and in scores of other nations around the world. But more often than not, the pioneer church planters are largely left on their own to figure out how to get the job done. A strong aversion to bureaucracy, control and standardization of polity have kept most new apostolic leaders from drawing up established principles and procedures for planting new churches and for managing the churches once they are planted.

Ted Haggard has now provided something that every new apostolic church leader has deeply desired: a practical operator's manual, so to speak, for starting and running a church. Many pastors and other church leaders within denominations have also wanted an answer to their question, How are these new fast-growing churches doing it? They will find their answer in *The Life-Giving Church*.

This book provides many practical lessons that are not usually taught in seminary, such as a chapter on etiquette: How do you restore the fallen? How do you take care of guest speakers? How do you hire and fire? Why are good manners so important?

I hope you don't miss the last chapter on bylaws. I know that very few will read it from beginning to end, but keep in mind that these are new apostolic bylaws and therefore quite different from *traditional* church bylaws. In new apostolic churches, however, it is assumed that the pastor is the *leader* of the church. There is a huge difference between the two mind-sets, and this is one of the first presentations of a model for new apostolic bylaws provided for church leaders in the form of a book.

I can personally affirm that the advice in *The Life-Giving Church* is good advice. This is not just because I have read and evaluated the book with professional church-growth eyes. Even more, it is because my wife, Doris, and I joined New Life Church when we moved from California to Colorado Springs. Ted Haggard is our pastor. I thought that our wonderful church in California would be hard to replace. But New Life Church has done it!

I have found an incredible presence of the Holy Spirit throughout the life of the church. I have found a passion for the nations of the world that could hardly be surpassed. I have found an incredible love for the community and its people. I have found spiritual freedom emerging from Pastor Ted's insistence that we live day by day under the tree of life as opposed to the tree of the knowledge of good and evil.

As you read this book, you will see what I mean. If you say "I want my church to be like that!" you will have made a good decision.

C. Peter Wagner
Chancellor, Wagner Leadership Institute

ACKNOWLEDGMENTS

This book reflects a lifetime of exposure to the church world and 15 years of personal experience as a senior pastor. During these years, my staff and I have accumulated ideas and materials from many sources. Our problem has been, though, that the vast majority of ideas within the church world sound good. But only by testing them by the Scriptures and through both personal and observed experiences can we determine which ones actually help.

So we're constantly observing great successes and, unfortunately, devastating failures because of contrasting ministry ideas. That's why I am grateful to the people listed below. They help me to think through issues and, as a result, have protected us from many hard lessons. I hope this book will do the same for you.

As you read *The Life-Giving Church*, our prayer is that it will help you avoid painful lessons and ease you into greater effectiveness in His kingdom. And, of course, I trust that it will inoculate you against bad ideas that would inadvertently limit the effectiveness of your ministry.

I believe in learning from others. It's less painful, and I like that. So the following are a few of the organizations and people who have contributed to the strengthening of the local church and have helped form some of the principles presented here:

- My wife, Gayle, and our five children, Christy, Marcus, Jonathan, Alex and Elliott. (If these ideas aren't perfected at home, then they don't work at church either.)
- New Life Church staff members: Ross Parsley, Lance Coles and John Bolin.
- Pastors Roy and Larry Stockstill of Bethany World Prayer Center, Baker, Louisiana.
- Dr. C. Peter and Doris Wagner, Wagner Leadership Institute, Colorado Springs, Colorado.
- Bob Sorge, Sally Morgenthaler and Kent Henry, all great worshipers.
- Martin Nussbaum, New Life Church legal counsel for policies and practices.
- The National Association of Evangelicals, Wheaton, Illinois.

CHAPTER ONE

MY FOUNDATION

So it is written: "The first man Adam became a living being"; the last Adam, a life-giving spirit.

1 CORINTHIANS 15:45

FIRST IMPRESSIONS

Delphi United Presbyterian Church is where Mom and Dad took me and my three older brothers to church while growing up on a farm in Indiana. My dad was the town veterinarian and owned several businesses and farms. At church, he was a presbyter and enjoyed teaching the high school Sunday School class. Mom did a remarkable job working at home. She had a home economics degree from Kansas State University in Manhattan, Kansas, the heartland of great food and strong families, and she was a professional at making our home and family a work of art. Whether hosting the women's missionary circle or preparing one of her great meals for our family, Mom was the best. And she and Dad decided the farm and the church would always be the center of our lives.

A few pictures of those years are indelibly imprinted on my mind, and those pictures form the values that shape my view of the local church. I can still see myself sobbing while sitting on the cold tile floor under the table in the basement Sunday School room with the teacher sympathetically pleading with me to come out. I can also see the four of us Haggard kids—Teddy, that's me, the youngest; Timmy, the strongest; Danny, the smartest; and Johnny, the oldest—sitting up straight in the pews with our starched white shirts, dark jackets and clip-on ties.

With our hair perfectly in place, fingernails trimmed and teeth freshly brushed, we stood tall, singing with hymnals in hand. The church seemed huge to me as a little boy, and I was proud of its giant stones, stained glass windows and towering ceilings. I was awed by the majesty of the pipe organ accompanying the beautifully robed choir. Each Sunday service was a model of worship and tidy Midwestern order.

We knew that if we poked, punched, whispered, laughed or did anything to draw attention to ourselves, Mom would gently glance at us, which was the first warning. Failure to adhere to the unspoken family rules would lead to the second warning, a gentle touch or soft pinch. After that, if we solicited even a giggle from another brother that distracted surrounding worshipers, there had better be a loving God in heaven who would help us, because we were going to receive some wholesome encouragement as soon as we got home.

So we didn't break the rules. Instead, we looked forward to the big family meals after church. Sometimes we would go to a little one-room restaurant on the highway that could seat a dozen or so people at a time. Mrs. Shick, the owner and chef, could make the best cheeseburgers, mashed potatoes and gravy, corn on the cob and green beans in the world. But most Sundays we would go home to an even better meal, usually of fried chicken, prepared by Mom. Sunday meals were always fun and loud, because we all wanted to eat and talk at the same time. I can still see Mom and Dad laughing hard with us during our Sunday dinners.

Delphi Presbyterian Church was the cornerstone of our family. It was the only time we were consistently formally dressed, starting with Saturday-night baths. Mom and Dad always made the routine of Sunday worship special. Mom called it the best day of the week. Throughout the week she would count the days until Sunday, which caused all of us to look forward to church.

Once, when I was six, everyone was so excited to get home for Sunday dinner that they left me at church. It's a childhood picture I hope I'll never forget: little Teddy Haggard standing on the church lawn crying, with family friends volunteering to drive me all the way to the Haggard farm. Then, when Daddy's Oldsmobile sped around the corner, I could see a look of relief on Mom and Dad's faces. But as the car approached, I could also see my three brothers laughing and pointing at me from the backseat. I was so embarrassed and angry that I jumped into the backseat with my brothers and tried to teach them a lesson by pounding on them. They just held me and kept laughing at me as I struggled—just what good, big, mean brothers are supposed to do.

These were my first impressions of what a church should be. Our family never considered not going to church. We never heard a negative word spoken about the pastor, the church or members of the community. Our parents wouldn't allow it. Negative judgment of others was not part of our culture.

I don't remember that the church service itself was ever anything spectacular. As I think about it, I don't know that we went because of the services. We went because we were Christians. Certainly, we never thought of the church as a place for entertainment or expected the church to keep us happy. Rather, it was a major focus of our lives because of the decisions Mom and Dad made about the kind of people they wanted us to associate with and the kind of people they wanted us to become.

Years later, when the Lord gave me the opportunity to pastor New Life, I was not particularly interested in building the church on events, entertainment or the most popular movement within the Body at the time. I enjoy those things very much, but the foundation of New Life is the Word and worship full of life and power; and it's intentionally structured to be a great place for parents to raise their children and to graciously mature together as a family. That idea came from Mom and Dad's unwavering consistency at Delphi United Presbyterian Church.

Another group of believers in Delphi that significantly impacted my impression of church was the Dunkers (so called for their method of baptism). They were actually Old German Baptist Brethren, but most people called them Amish. Like the Amish, they lived simple rural lifestyles, without electricity in their homes, and used horses and buggies for transportation.

I was vividly aware of the Dunkers because they traveled to and from town on the road in front of our house. The largest Dunker family, the Royers, would stop from time to time to visit with Mom and Dad. Dad was their veterinarian and felt very protective of their community because they were completely nonviolent. I remember hearing Dad on the phone telling people that it was our responsibility to protect them so they would have a safe place to farm and raise their families. We were probably as close to the Royers as any non-Amish family could be. Living near them and knowing them gave me an opportunity to see their humility and sincere faith.

One night a group of drunken high school boys went out to the Royer farm after a football game and began breaking watermelons—the produce that provided the mainstay of their annual income. While the boys were yelling and cussing in the field, the light of a glowing lantern began flickering in an upstairs bedroom of the farmhouse. From the field the boys could see the light being carried down the stairs and then out onto the front porch. As the light approached them through the darkness, the boys prepared for a fight. Instead, Mr. Royer told the boys they could have all the melons they desired, but that the melons they were breaking were not his best. He offered to lead them to the best field and give them as many as they wanted.

The boys were embarrassed and respectfully apologized before leaving. Mr. Royer invited them in for a glass of lemonade—he said they needed it. But the boys declined, trying to soak in their vivid lesson on Christian character.

The Royers influenced many people. Instead of preaching with words, they communicated by living well. They would never argue over material possessions, never judge another or ever knowingly cause another to sin. That's why their homes were simple, their clothing plain and their speech soft and kind.

The Dunkers loved the Bible and actually practiced the Scriptures. They would never dream of resisting an evil man, rebelling against authority or flaunting anything that might stir envy in another's heart. They believed that heaven was their home. Alcoholism, sexually transmitted diseases, divorce, violence and betrayal were unheard of in their community. The Dunkers were models of godly character and conviction for me.

BEING A CHRISTIAN MEANS THAT THE REALITY OF HEAVEN AFFECTS EVERY AREA OF OUR LIVES.

When I think of a Christian community, I think of the honesty, the generosity and the adherence to Scripture of the Royer family. Because of that influence, I would never think of causing others to have to lock their cars, homes or businesses because of my presence. Being a Christian means that the reality of heaven affects every area of our lives, and that we stop struggling against one another in order to gain the wisdom to work together in harmony and trust. I believe all Christians can embrace these values. Rural cultures don't produce these values, holy hearts do. And Jesus' holiness is available to all of us, no matter where we live—that's what should be evident in our churches.

In Delphi, the back doors of businesses were left unlocked in case someone needed something. Daddy used to go into businesses after hours to pick up an item and leave the money and a note on the cash register so the owner would know exactly what he had purchased. Stealing was never considered. To take something you hadn't earned was shameful. The fabric of our community was woven with trust, honesty and a meaningful handshake. Caring for each other's children and humbly sacri-ficing for another person's good was the norm, not the excep-tion.

As I write these first impressions of church and Christian people, I realize things couldn't have been as ideal as I remember them. I'm 44 now, and I know better. However, I think it's great that these are the memories from the eyes of little Teddy Haggard. I want my kids to have memories just as wholesome. It makes adult life easier.

And that's precisely why we need good churches—life-giving churches.

Truth Versus Religious Institutions

When I was in the seventh grade, our world began to change. Daddy's back started to bother him, making it impossible for him to work. Even though his friends tried to help, Dad's pain was so intense that he had to lie on a hard wooden surface with-out moving. We were forced to begin selling farm and other assets. The laughter in our home became much less frequent.

At some point during this period, Dad saw Billy Graham on television. For the first time in his life, Dad heard about being born again. After praying with Graham, Dad went to talk with our pastor, who told him that the term "born again" was irrelevant to our modern culture and didn't have any contemporary applica-tion. Our pastor warned Dad not to expose our family or his Sunday School class to anyone who believed in being born again.

Even though various people within the community offered to help our family, our financial condition worsened. Dad couldn't stand the thought of borrowing from people in our community, so in the midst of the dichotomy of his spiritual renewal and horrible back pain, he and Mom decided to move us to a larger community where they could build a small veterinary practice that would be easier on Dad's back.

When we moved, Dad found an evangelical church with a pastor who understood being born again. But because of his previous experience in our former church, Dad felt compelled to read and trust in what he read in his own Bible. While we were settling into our new church home, Dad read about being filled with the Holy Spirit. He asked our new pastor about it and was told not to pursue this experience because it might lead him into fanaticism.

Then, while praying about some of the Scriptures, Dad had a powerful encounter with the Holy Spirit. But because our new pastor had discouraged his seeking this wonderful experience, Dad began to doubt the spiritual integrity of our new church as well. Once again, we moved on.

Eventually, Dad started associating with a group of believers who emphasized the gifts and the power of God's Holy Spirit—a major cultural move for our family. While worshiping with this group, Dad discovered the Scriptures about deliverance. Because of some old negative patterns that had been deeply rooted in the Haggard family, Dad was very interested in personal deliverance. When he asked his new friends about it, they said Christians never need deliverance, only sanctification. They discouraged him from associating with anyone who believed that Christians could be candidates for deliverance. Dad and I and some other family members did eventually receive our much-needed deliverance from generations of bondage, but unfortunately, once again, people connected with institutional religion had attempted to thwart our family's growth in the Scriptures and in the power of God.

MY PASTORAL CALL

When God called me into pastoral ministry, I was concerned about how Dad would respond. He had become suspicious of church structures and pastors. I was home from college after my freshman year as a telecommunications major with a minor in journalism. It was late, and I was by myself in the kitchen, pouring a bowl of cereal, when God spoke into my spirit and called me. I was totally surprised.

I paused, smiled, and told the Lord I wanted to serve Him. But before I mentioned this to anyone, especially to my parents, I asked the Lord to assure me by using others to confirm His calling on my life. I felt as though He consented, so I went into the living room to watch TV and eat Cheerios.

The next morning I received a letter from Curry Juneau, my Sunday School teacher at the church I attended while away at college. Curry wrote that he had been asked by another church to become its senior pastor and that he would accept the position if I would agree to join him as the youth pastor. I grinned as I read the letter. *Confirmation number one.*

Later that same day, Pastor Jeff Floyd, one of the pastors eulogized in the dedication of this book, dropped by the house. He had come to ask if I planned to be in church on Sunday. When I said yes, Jeff was pleased because he said the deacons had voted to license me into the ministry so I could officially begin preparations to be a pastor. They had never spoken to me about this, nor had I hinted at any interest. But Jeff smiled broadly as he told me what they had already decided to do. *Confirmation number two.*

Then, that evening, Owen Crankshaw, one of my buddies from high school, came by to pick me up to go out for some fun. As we drove, Owen asked me why I was a telecommunications major when I was going to be a pastor. *Confirmation number three.*

That did it! Pastoral work had never been a subject with my friends before, and yet, after one quick encounter with the Holy Spirit in the kitchen, over a bowl of cereal, it seemed everyone knew more than I did about my calling.

But I was cautious about telling Dad that God had spoken to me about becoming a pastor because three respected pastors had given him advice that was contrary to Scripture. Even though I had received three supernatural confirmations, I knew I would not violate my dad's counsel. In my mind, I kept hearing him say, *Most traditional churches are worldly institutions that appease God's people and keep them from knowing the Scriptures or the power of God.* Dad no longer trusted pastors to be godly men of integrity, and now I wanted to be one.

The next day, I was working in Dad's office and decided to tell him what had happened to me. When I told him, he dropped his head to think, looked up at me, and said he believed God had indeed called me. Then he cautioned: "If worldly church systems or politics ever begin to drain God's life out of you, you must get out quickly. Don't let others kill it." I gave him my word and he gave me his blessing. *Confirmation number four.*

SEEDS OF APOSTOLIC MINISTRY

The next Sunday, I was licensed at Yorktown Baptist Church and then I returned to school as a sophomore. Upon my return, I switched my major to biblical literature with a Christian education minor and began working with Curry Juneau at Phoenix Avenue Baptist Church. While at Phoenix Avenue, I also served as chaplain, Spiritual Life Dorm Director and led summer missions teams to complete my degree. It was on a summer missions trip in 1977 that the Lord first spoke to me about what I now understand to be the apostolic influence.

Our team was ministering in Washington D.C., and we took a day off to tour the city. Near the end of the day, we decided to visit the Capitol. It was late in the evening and very few people were around. I wandered into the basement and there, directly under the dome, were display cases with a small raised circle in the middle. I walked over and stood on the circle; and the power of God came on me and said, "If you will obey me, your ministry influence will reach as many people as this building influences." I didn't tell anyone, but I knew that God loved me and wanted to use me to serve others.

LOCAL CHURCHES WITH A GLOBAL VISION

As graduation approached, I was hired by World Missions for Jesus, a West German missions organization, to become their American representative. World Missions worked exclusively to assist the believers behind the Iron Curtain and in Third World socialistic countries. The risks that believers were taking to assist other believers suffering under Communist dictatorships gave me personal insight into the universal Body of Christ, the importance of Christians working in harmony together and the inevitable tragic results whenever Christians separate themselves from one another.

After a year and a half with World Missions, I became the American vice president, which was more administration than I liked. So I resigned from World Missions and joined the ministry team at Bethany Baptist Church, which is now Bethany

World Prayer Center, in Baker, Louisiana. During the five years at Bethany, my wife, Gayle, and I learned many of the principles for a life-giving church that are in this book. Those principles are:

- Rest.
- Keep your word.
- Don't think more highly of yourself than you ought.
- Churches are to care for others.
- Strong leadership combined with consistency, humility and honesty builds healthy churches.
- Churches are healthiest when not swayed too soon by Christian movements.
- Keep no secrets.

COLORADO SPRINGS

After working with Bethany for five years, Gayle and I thought we would serve there all of our lives. But while on vacation in Colorado Springs, visiting Gayle's family, our lives changed forever. I took a pup tent, a gallon of water, Scripture cassettes and my Bible to the back of Pikes Peak to pray and fast for three days. On that trip, God spoke to me about Colorado Springs and called me to pastor there.

While praying and fasting, I saw four things:

1. A stadium full of men worshiping God (there were no children or women, but huge numbers of men worshiping God);
2. A place where people could pray and fast for revival in Colorado Springs without any distractions;

3. People being connected from all over the world to pray
   for the lost through a world prayer center containing
   a huge globe;
4. A church where people could freely worship God and
   study the Scriptures with no strings attached. A hassle-
   free, life-giving church.

I was not very familiar with visions. As I thought about what I
had seen, I remembered the one previous vision God had given me.

I was a high school student attending Yorktown Baptist
Church, and because I loved to go to church and pray, the pastor
had given me a key to the building. One afternoon as I was walking through the church and praying, I saw a delivery room in a
hospital. In the center of the room were the usual lights and
equipment necessary to deliver babies, but around the walls were
spirits. I could see them clearly. Some were tall and strong; others were like nervous animals. Some were confident; others were
hyperactive.

As the hospital attendants brought pregnant women into
the delivery room and the doctors and nurses would deliver a
baby, the strongest, most dominant demon would assign a
demon to the baby. Sometimes the assigned demon would go
into the baby's body; other times the demon would just hover
around the baby and follow as the baby was carried out of the
delivery room. Time after time, a demon was assigned to each
baby who was newly delivered.

As each demon was assigned, I intuitively knew its assign-
ment: to instill or addict the person to hate, drugs, immorality,
self-centeredness, high-mindedness, greed, manipulation, lying,
rebellion, masturbation, pornography, witchcraft, idolatry, etc.
The spirits were assigned to keep these kids from knowing
Christ and to ruin their lives.

After seeing this, I had greater understanding of spiritual activity and the meaning of the Scripture in 1 Corinthians 7 about the faith of the parents sanctifying the lives of their children. If the parents were believers, the spirit went with them but did not enter them—they would only whisper to them. If the parents were not believers, the demon would enter the child and integrate into his or her personality.

This vision powerfully impacted the way I prayed and lived; so when I saw the four visions on Pikes Peak, I knew God was again speaking something profound to me. I knew He had a very specific plan, and I knew He had shown me something that I needed to be a part of in Colorado Springs.

My life's direction changed. In addition to praying about Baton Rouge and the ministry there, I started praying with increased spiritual authority for God to raise up young men and women from Colorado Springs to go into the world, that God would attract wholesome parachurch ministries to the city and that He would raise up strong and healthy life-giving churches that would have apostolic authority, influence and vision.

Even though I didn't know if God would use me physically to do any of these things, I knew I had experienced the heart of God and that I needed to pray and be available to Him.

All four of those visions have come to pass. In the case of the men in stadiums, I haven't had any direct involvement. In the other three, I have had direct involvement.

- The first vision was fulfilled when Coach Bill McCartney received the same idea about 10 years later as he was driving through Colorado Springs. That ministry is Promise Keepers.
- The second vision is Praise Mountain, a prayer and fasting center in Florissant, Colorado, where people have

been continuously praying and fasting for our city since
1987.

• The third vision is The World Prayer Center in Colorado Springs.

• The fourth vision is New Life Church.

When Gayle and I came to Colorado Springs in August of 1984, we had been blessed with positive church experiences. Neither of us had ever been involved with a church split, a mishandled moral failure, broken or wounded spirits because of betrayal or deception, or any other heartbreaking local church problems. Because of our history, we knew God had given us great models for ministry. We also knew that if we could just pastor the way we had seen others pastor, we could successfully serve people for many years.

In the late fall of 1984, missionary-apostle Danny Ost, from Mexico City, came to Colorado Springs to help me prepare the birthing of New Life Church. Danny was an old-fashioned apostle (I fondly refer to him as a Paul type of apostle). He founded hundreds of churches, saw incredible miracles and preached to more people every weekend than anyone else in the world during those days except Dr. Cho in Seoul, South Korea (who pastors the world's largest church). Ost deposited an apostolic anointing on our church as he spent time helping us prepare to launch the church.

On the first Sunday in January 1985, New Life Church was birthed with a handful of people in the basement of our recently purchased home. God blessed us with immediate growth, and five months later we moved into our first public space—a little auditorium that seated 200 people and had a small room for a nursery and children's ministry.

After one meeting in that small strip mall location, nestled between a bar and a liquor store, some men from the church asked me to come into a small side room and get on my knees. As they prayed for me, I opened my eyes and saw them placing a towel on the floor in front of me. Then they poured a quart (I'm not kidding!) of oil on my head to anoint me for our next step. It came quickly!

In May 1986, we moved down the street to a larger building. We reconstructed the inside of the building into a 650-seat auditorium with room for a few classrooms and offices. In 1987, Paul and Geri Fix, from Florissant, Colorado, gave the church a 70-acre field as a seed toward Praise Mountain, the prayer and fasting center. The church bought two adjacent pieces of property, which resulted in a beautiful 110-acre facility where people pray and fast to this day.

The next seed of apostolic grace was planted by Pastor Bernie Kuiper from Village Seven Presbyterian Church in Colorado Springs. I was praying in our church auditorium when I felt like God told me that Pastor Kuiper was the bishop of Colorado Springs and that I needed to meet him.

Well, that was a tall order. I was a 28-year-old Spirit-filled Baptist, pastoring an independent charismatic church in a storefront. Bernie Kuiper was a respected reformed/cessationist Presbyterian pastor of a well-established church who was known for his anti-charismatic standing. I was shocked at God! But because I had attended Bill Gothard's Basic Youth Conflicts seminar, I knew the importance of the blessing from those in spiritual authority. So I called for an appointment. Pastor Kuiper met me, questioned me for one hour about my theology and ended up laying his hands on me and praying that God would "give him the largest church in the city." Now that has happened—his prayer has been answered. I believe Bernie Kuiper's blessing launched New Life into the next expansion.

In May 1988, the congregation moved into a larger store-front that was constructed into a 1,500-seat auditorium with a small youth chapel, 12 classrooms and a small office space. That building, like the others before, was quickly filled to capacity, but we couldn't find a space in the city large enough to hold the expanding congregation. It was time to buy land and build.

Because of our strong missions philosophy and our deter-mination not to be wasteful or ostentatious, the church sought land in the county, which had to be annexed to the city before construction could proceed. In 1991, New Life Church pur-chased 35 rural acres on Highway 83 and constructed a simple concrete structure. The new building had an auditorium that would seat as many as 4,000, with limited classroom and office space. The first service was held Christmas night, December 25, 1991.

Then, in early 1992, my world took a new shape. I received a fax from Danny Ost's son, Tim, in Mexico City, telling me to meet him in Upland, California, for a very important meeting. He didn't say what it was, but I knew and respected Tim, so I went.

When I arrived, I met Luis Bush, Dick Eastman, Peter and Doris Wagner and several other recognized leaders. From that meeting, New Life Church formed its mission for the 1990s—to support Luis Bush generally and Peter and Doris Wagner specif-ically to build a network of prayer for the lost—a calling that led to the creation of the World Prayer Center and much more. We as a team coordinated the Prayer Through the Window series that had 22,500,000 participants in 1993; 36,700,000 partici-pants in 1995; over 40,000,000 in 1997; and the same in 1999. It was in the midst of these global prayer efforts that Peter Wagner made the transition from seeing himself as a seminary professor to a person with an apostolic call who would convene people so they could effectively reach the darkest areas in the world (this is described in Peter's book *Apostles and Prophets: The Foundation of the Church*).

During that same period, my life took on refined spiritual definition as well. In 1993, during our first prayer journey, we went to Israel, and our guide took us to a cemetery on the Mount of Olives where many first-century Christians are buried. He said they were buried there because they believed this was the spot where Jesus ascended to heaven (seems to me that they would know!). Even though this wasn't the officially recognized spot, I went into the cemetery and, while standing alone, the Holy Spirit came on me and said, "You are my David of this generation. If you'll obey me, my grace will rest on you without measure. My favor in you will give you your generation if you want it. From this spot, I changed the world. From this spot, you are empowered to begin."

From that time until now, apostolic power has blessed me. My only problems are with me—not with the enemy, not with circumstances, not with people.

The Wagners and the Bushes moved to Colorado Springs and became active in New Life Church. AD 2000 and Beyond was a blessing to the world. The World Prayer Center was built and dedicated in 1998 and now hosts the Association of Local Church Prayer Leaders, Global Harvest Ministries, Wagner Leadership Institute, Wagner Publications and 24-hour-a-day worship and intercession for the nations.

New Life now has over 7,000 members. Because of our emphasis on missions, the church gave more than $2 million to missions last year (1999). We pray that this kind of giving will continue to increase.

Thus, my foundations for the life-giving church. The value of life-giving churches starts for me in Delphi, Indiana, with the

Presbyterians and the Dunkers. The values learned there, my dad's warning to avoid draining religious structures and to trust the Scriptures, Bethany World Prayer Center's emphasis on integrity and God's seeds of apostolic anointing were fundamental to my personal development. These elements convinced me that church could and should be simple, effective, innovative and empowering.

I used to think we were somewhat unique; then I learned that life-giving churches all around the world have discovered how to practice freedom, trust, spiritual sensitivity and honesty in a simple format. In fact, innovative life-giving churches are the fastest-growing churches in the world. The negative realities of the "god business" cause me to cling to the simplicity of the life-giving church. Certainly, not all life-giving churches are the same—many are more established and are of various sizes, but all of them emphasize the power of God, the integrity of the Scriptures and the life available in Christ.

I believe we need healthy, life-giving apostolic churches to disciple people, to raise up the next generation

THE NEGATIVE REALITIES OF THE "GOD BUSINESS" CAUSE ME TO CLING TO THE SIMPLICITY OF THE LIFE-GIVING CHURCH.

and to complete the Great Commission. Passive, permission-withholding churches will not do. Without a doubt, the apostolic strength that God is highlighting will not have the platform it needs without healthy life-giving churches. And I believe the prophetic voice God is manifesting right now will not be properly acted upon without healthy life-giving churches.

This is my plea: Read this book with your heart and mind keenly open to His plan for the next generation. Tomorrow is coming no matter what; yesterday will never return. Our churches are for His work today and tomorrow. This is the time to build.

CHAPTER TWO

YOUNG DAVIDS: MOBILIZING A GENERATION

Each one should use whatever gift he has received to serve others,
faithfully administering God's grace in its various forms.

1 PETER 4:10

SOMETHING IS WRONG

Life-giving churches attract people who love God but do not necessarily like the church world very much. I can relate. Sometimes I'm like that. I love the Bible; I seek the manifestations of the Holy Spirit; I enjoy the diversity of the Body and look forward to His Second Coming. Believers make me smile. Prayer is a delight; spiritual warfare is exhilarating; serving others is deeply satisfying. I am thrilled when I think of a good small group. I like studying the Bible, going on Christian retreats and participating in powerful worship services. To me they're fun, because they give me life.

But when many people think of church, they don't think of the life-giving experience that comes from knowing Christ. Instead they think of excessive introspection, irrelevant sermons and appeals for money. For many people, baptisms, weddings and funerals are the only purposes a church serves. These same people draw security from knowing that Grandma goes to church; but when they think of what churches stand for, they want to avoid them. No one ever says, "I want to have a great party at my house this Friday. Let's invite all the pastors and church elders!" Nope. Doesn't happen. Why? Because too often churches make nice people mean, happy people sad and innovative people want to pull their hair out. Something is wrong on the main street of traditional church structures.

What Has to Change and Why

We have learned a great deal about spiritual freedom in the last 30 years and gained fresh insight into the work of the Holy Spirit, deliverance and signs and wonders. But now we're seeing that our past structures do not provide the freedom that our newfound spiritual strength requires. We need both spiritual and structural freedom to embrace and create the changes that must come. If we will take it, we have the opportunity to enjoy spiritual freedom and build corresponding church structures that provide structural freedom as well.

Another opportunity that has crystallized in the last 10 years is the quantification of the remaining task of the Great Commission. In 1995, Christian delegates from virtually every nation on Earth congregated in Seoul, South Korea, for what was called a Global Consultation of World Evangelization. As a result of this consultation, we now have better lists and strategies for the unreached people groups and the least evangelized people groups. We now know where they are, what they look like, what languages they speak, and we have information on their cultures. Thus, we know for the first time in 2,000 years the scope of the remaining task, and we understand how to approach it.

Denominations, churches and servant ministries can now easily make a difference in the task of ensuring that the gospel is available to every person on Earth in his own language and culture within our lifetime. In the past, efforts were random at best. Now we know how to strategically advance, and we know how to measure our impact.

A third opportunity is a logical follow-up to the others: the need for apostolic advance. If we are to use our new freedom and resources well, we need the same anointing the Early Church enjoyed with Paul and the other apostles in order to advance into dark areas and establish and serve local churches. Certainly we need structures, accountability, chain of command and job descriptions. But using these tools without apostolic leadership and prophetic insight can be well-intentioned but shallow attempts to perform a spiritual function with natural strength.

Please understand that I believe we need natural strength and systems to get things done; but to do what we need to do on Earth in our generation, we also need life-giving churches with apostolic strength.

I, like many of you, have a number of hesitations with certain aspects of the increased attention now being given to apostolic and prophetic growth. I think our hesitation mainly has to do with knowing "apostles" who have been failures in their local churches; that is, some of those who call themselves apostles are church ministers who were unsuccessful or unable to successfully disciple people on a local level. Their new title has given them an escape from the responsibility of honorably discipling the people with whom they were already in relationship.

The same is true with the prophetic. When we keep hearing about false prophets and inaccurate prophecies, and when we have to help people struggle through hearing prophets explain why their prophecies didn't come true, it's tempting to discard the prophetic.

We must not do that. We must not disavow our prophets and apostles because of a few unfortunate missteps. We must distinguish between what is good about apostolic and prophetic leadership, and what is false. Just as there are incompetent and dishonest pastors, teachers and evangelists, so there are people calling themselves apostles and prophets who are not working out of the supernatural strength of the Holy Spirit. But we can learn to tell the good from the bad. We can evaluate the genuineness of people's roles by examining how they minister in local churches and work with the same people day after day. Some may not want this scrutiny, but I think it was the pattern set by the New Testament apostles and prophets—they were faithful to their duties at the local church.

Completely discarding the apostolic and prophetic because of some fallibility would be no different from discarding electricity because someone got shocked. We must recognize the need to know God's voice and grow in the strength of the apostolic and prophetic. We don't have to coddle foolishness, but we do want to build on the strength of God's plan of advance for our generation.

Mobilizing Today's Christian Ministries

The November 1996 issue of *Christianity Today* profiled 50 people, age 40 or younger, who demonstrated leadership potential for the next generation of evangelicalism. I was one of those 50. I found it interesting that only nine of us ministered primarily through local church structures. Some of the reasons were obvious: One person was a congressman and others were journalists, musicians, educators and professional athletes. Based on the discussions we had when we met at the 1997 National Association of Evangelicals convention, the rest of the group discovered that even though they loved their local churches and felt a part of the local Body, they could not adequately minister through the local church structure. And, for all the reasons already mentioned, they were right.

The Lord is changing the structures He is using to mobilize Christian ministry. Many of us closely associated with local churches are rapidly embracing the changes that are driven by emerging megachurches and servant ministries. One indicator of this change is that seminaries—our traditional training system for Christian leaders—are no longer the exclusive training centers for the leaders of many of our most successful churches or successful servant ministries. Focus on the Family was founded and is prospering under the leadership of Dr. James Dobson, a child psychologist; Promise Keepers was founded and is being directed by Bill McCartney, a football coach.

I have been a guest lecturer for the doctor of ministry classes at both Fuller Seminary and Oral Roberts University. In both of those settings, some of the students were already national and international leaders who had chosen to return to school to earn their doctorates. It wasn't formal training that made these people successful; it was their success that highlighted their need for training.

Interestingly enough, several of the students commented to me that one major benefit of returning to school was the interaction in class with their peers. They wanted to learn from each other. This system of ministry practitioners who teach each other works, which is why many megachurches have their own leadership training institutes and why Peter Wagner formed Wagner Leadership Institute (WLI) here in Colorado Springs, which provides bachelor's, master's, and doctorate-level studies led by practitioners—for other practitioners.

Though I have a deep appreciation for informal training, we at New Life still require all salaried employees to have at least a bachelor's degree. We appreciate the value of academic education in conjunction with a strong apprentice relationship with a practitioner in order to model successful ministry. I believe that healthy life-giving churches need a good mix of both approaches (academic and practical) to stimulate new leadership styles.

I don't intend to comment here on the benefits or consequences of the evolving sources of our Christian leadership. But it is notable that new technical terms are being developed to describe the emerging systems. Peter Wagner regularly writes and speaks about the "new apostolic reformation." He has accurately recognized the changes as so dramatic that they are creating an actual reformation within the Body of Christ. Without question, we are improving the way we administrate churches and how churches relate to one another.

Dr. Wagner's book *Churchquake* is a recent publication that describes the evolving way we administrate the discipling of believers through local churches. I think that every pastor and church leader should consider the ideas in this book.

Not only are we improving the way we train leaders, but we are also changing the way that congregations relate to one another. Several years ago I wrote in *Primary Purpose* about the new ways that coalitions of churches are working together to promote more aggressive conversion growth in their cities. As a follow-up book, Jack Hayford and I coauthored *Loving Your City into the Kingdom* with Bill Bright, George Barna, Tony Evans and others to explain how churches can work together to affect their entire city.

Obviously, the Holy Spirit is birthing this dramatic change. The public is seeking out churches that minister abundant living, and servant ministries that strategically advance Christ's kingdom. This public demand is forcing rapid changes in existing organizations that desire to grow, and new organizations are being birthed from innovation and creativity.

These days we seldom look to traditional church hierarchies to teach us how to do church. Instead, we look to those on the cutting edge—the thoughtful innovators who are creative and spiritually daring, with proven successes. Even though some of these leaders hesitate to identify their influence as apostolic, I see them that way. I believe Rick Warren, Tommy Barnett, Larry Stockstill, Bill Hybels, T. D. Jakes and many others have an apostolic anointing on their lives, and God has used them to establish apostolic churches in order to rapidly advance His Kingdom.

Each of these leaders has a specific sphere of influence. Even though their respective denominations often do not know how to relate to and administrate the spiritual influence of these men and others of their type, thousands of pastors look to them for spiritual guidance and practical coaching in ministry. They are apostles.

I understand the hesitation to use the word "apostle," but we shouldn't hesitate to accurately identify and respond to "apostolic anointing and function." That is, I think it would be wise for pastors in Phoenix to listen very closely to Tommy Barnett. Pastors in Los Angeles should listen to Jack Hayford. Pastors in Baton Rouge need to honor Larry Stockstill, and so on. These men are pioneers. They are great thinkers. They know something unusual. They know how to do ministry and should be respected as apostles even though they (and others who are uncomfortable with the term "apostle") will probably always call themselves pastors.

Notice that the platform for these apostolic ministries is the life-giving church. I'm not saying that all apostolic ministry should be structured like these churches, but all apostolic ministry must prove itself in the day-to-day life of the local church, not just in conferences, books or programs.

PRESERVING OUR DAVIDS AND INFANT KINGS

Because of improved communication within the Body of Christ, we can find those who know how to most effectively minister life and learn from them. Our entrepreneurs and innovators are rising to the surface, and when they do, we hear about them. That's why I was so fascinated with the 50 people chosen by *Christianity Today*. They are certainly a promising group; and no one knows which of these people will actually make a positive contribution to the growth of evangelicalism.

Christianity Today's article implied that there are many people who are not on the list because they are currently unnoticed shepherds. Many of these young men and women are in local churches, trying to find the mystery of true ministry while serving as youth pastors, music ministers, assistant pastors, cell leaders or volunteers. They love the purpose of the church. My concern is that when the church bogs down in gossip and inefficiency, they will go where the water flows more freely—outside the local church.

Young Davids—future leaders of the Church—want structures that facilitate relationships that are conduits for His living water and provide sustenance from the Bread of Life. But if true life is secondary to a well-intentioned but top-heavy bureaucratic structure that appears political, corrupt or hurts people, then our Davids will graciously excuse themselves.

To stimulate greater opportunity within our local churches for Davids of every age is one of the reasons this book was written. Our future will be brighter when they have a positive experience within their local church structures rather than, like so many other infant kings, being poisoned before they ever approach notable service.

Retaining the Brightest and Best for Kingdom Work

When considering the young Davids, I can't help but think of Bill Gates's book *The Road Ahead*, which emphasizes the necessity of building a corporate atmosphere that attracts and retains the brightest and the best of the business—the entrepreneurs. Gates says that the greatest threat to Microsoft is not NCR, Hewlett Packard, Ford Electronics or IBM, but some college student in a dormitory somewhere playing on his or her laptop

YOUNG DAVIDS—

FUTURE LEADERS

OF THE

CHURCH—WANT

STRUCTURES

TO FACILITATE

RELATIONSHIPS

THAT ARE

CONDUITS FOR

HIS LIVING

WATER.

computer—a David. Gates maintains that these Davids are learning what the major corporations already know, but they are developing better ideas than paid researchers and developers usually generate.

His concern is that these innovators will get out of school, go to work for Microsoft for a few years and then branch off and start a competing organization that is highly focused in a particular field. That new organization, driven with the creative innocence of the young David, will probably provide a better product at a better price than Microsoft, the large established corporation.

So Gates is taking strong action now. Microsoft's foresight requires it to provide a healthy corporate structure that is not threatened by or passively hostile toward the entrepreneurs, but rather embraces its Davids, causing the entrepreneurs to want to stay within Microsoft. Then Microsoft will become stronger because of a corporate environment that values the changes birthed by creative innovators. Bill Gates wants the Davids of the microelectronics business to stay, just as we want the Davids of the Body of Christ to be productive within our local churches, not driven from them.

Most young Davids within the Christian world start with an innocent heart before God and a trusting attitude toward churches. But when they discover cumbersome systems and unnecessary processes that don't contribute to effective ministry, these disillusioned Davids quickly decide they can do more elsewhere. Therefore, our local churches may unnecessarily be losing some of our brightest and best future leaders.

It's no wonder that while we have more money, buildings, books, seminars, seminaries and support groups than ever, 80 percent of our North American churches have either plateaued or are declining. While the Body of Christ is growing three times faster than the population growth rate globally, why hasn't the North American Church experienced any net growth in more than 20 years? I think one reason has something to do with how our Davids are being treated within our local church structures. Fortunately, we are changing.

Too often, church structures restrain godliness and inadvertently provide a voice for ungodliness. We've all grimaced when our structures have unnecessarily given platform to the whiners, manipulators and controllers within the Body, while our strongest innovators gently begin moving toward the door because they don't need to tolerate unnecessary and unproductive systems.

We have a paradox here. The message of the gospel provides spiritual freedom, but our local church structures too often steal our innocence and produce bondage, slowly draining us of the very spiritual life and joy we are supposed to minister to others. We can fix this problem. Actually, we must, or we may become like our predecessors: whitewashed tombs looking good on the outside but powerless and maybe even dead on the inside.

There is no reason to allow these repressive, encumbering systems to continue to drive the church. What are we protecting? Small bastions of a culture that were squeezed out of mainstream society years ago? Our local churches can be spiritual powerhouses of effective ministry *to people*. They should be stable, but not so stable that they are dead. Therefore, our churches must provide simple structures that are tracks for effective ministry rather than restrictive barriers. In the midst of America's spiral away from its Judeo-Christian foundation, God is preparing strong leaders with creative dreams and aspirations for the next generation of local churches in order to reverse this negative trend.

Attracting and retaining our future leaders within existing local church structures will require some risks as we rearrange the ways we minister with and to our congregations. Certainly, we need the necessary checks and balances to prevent abuse. But we must also recognize that those who have the greatest potential require the freedom to test their wings in order to either fly or fall. If we protect them too much from falling, that same over-protection may keep them from flying. Then we are stuck with more status quo and no net growth in plateaued local churches. We can't afford this any longer. We need to make the transition to the life-giving church.

CHAPTER THREE

LIVING IN THE TREE OF LIFE

On each side of the river stood the tree of life, bearing twelve crops of fruit, yielding its fruit every month. And the leaves of the tree are for the healing of the nations.

REVELATION 22:2

THE LIFE-GIVING HOLY SPIRIT

Mrs. Morgan has been enjoying the Body of Christ from the same pew of Saint Peter's practically every Sunday for more than 30 years. The slope in the wood grain eternally marks the exact location from which this faithful church secretary observes weddings, funerals, baptisms and children fidgeting in their seats. For decades, she has been watching people move in and out of town, children grow up and marry and parents become grandparents. From her pew she watches widows grieve for their departed spouses and children's choirs sing special songs at Christmas. Mrs. Morgan faithfully teaches her Sunday School class and pitches in at picnics, community outreaches and special programs.

At times the church has been healthy and growing with the strength of young people and an atmosphere created by bustling families. Other times the church has felt tired and solemn. But Mrs. Morgan has never wavered. She loves her church. And so do the rest of the people of Saint Peter's. Almost without fail, Saint Peter's is filled with people who love to pitch in and help one another. They aren't problem-free—they just enjoy one another and enjoy worshiping and serving God together.

Just a few minutes' drive from Saint Peter's is another church of the same denomination. Even though the theology is the same and the people are from the same neighborhood, the church feels different. For some mysterious reason, people fight easily in that church. They are contentious, defensive, and often demanding. The pastor seems dissatisfied, and the staff seems uncertain. The atmosphere is the exact opposite of Saint Peter's—prickly rather than warm; awkward rather than welcoming.

What's the difference? Though the churches believe and teach the same thing, one gives life, the other does not. Why is that?

When we use the term "life-giving" in the context of church ministry, we're talking about churches that teach people to receive the life of God, available through faith in Jesus. Theoretically, all churches that believe in the Lord Jesus Christ and the message of the Bible are life-giving.

Unfortunately, however, we all know churches that believe the same basic things we do, and yet their problems seem overwhelming. The pastors fight with each other. The members seem mean-spirited. Gossip and rumors have replaced meaningful conversation. The people seem opinionated and empty. Church programs and small groups never seem to work out.

What's the problem? How can one church that teaches salvation in the Lord Jesus have full Sunday School classes, be populated with smiling people and experience real growth, while another church that teaches the very same thing struggles to survive?

A Snake, a Garden and a Choice

Years ago, the Lord taught me a simple lesson from the creation account in Genesis that helped me to see the difference between churches (and people) that are life-giving and those that are not.

You will remember that God had made the Garden of Eden plentiful with everything necessary for a wonderful life. In the middle of the garden were the tree of life and the tree of the knowledge of good and evil (see Gen. 2:9). When God set Adam and Eve in the garden, he told them they were free to eat anything and everything except for the fruit of one tree—the tree of the knowledge of good and evil. "You must not eat from [it]," God says, "for when you eat of it you will surely die" (v. 17).

Of course, the serpent quickly came and convinced Eve to eat the fruit of the forbidden tree, telling her, "You will not surely die . . . for God knows that when you eat of it your eyes will be opened, and you will be like God, knowing good and evil" (Gen. 3:4,5). Notice that he did not encourage Eve to rebel; he appealed to her love for God and desire to be more like Him. He offered her an appearance of godliness, but one that was actually devoid of life.

The choice offered to Eve is the same choice we are offered today. We can choose to live according to the knowledge of good and evil, maintaining a form of godliness and a certain righ-teousness (but one that will ultimately leave us cold and dark), or we can choose to eat from the tree of life and discover godli-ness and righteousness naturally through our relationship with the Lord Jesus Christ.

Different Trees, Different Fruit

Then Jesus declared, "I am the bread of life" (John 6:35).

To eat something is to ingest it, to take its qualities into yourself, to make it a part of you. When we eat, we are taking something that is outside ourselves, absorbing it and utilizing it for our own use. That's why eating is such a useful metaphor for read-ing, watching television, listening to teachers or engaging in dis-cussion. In all those actions, we are consuming knowledge and ideas, and those ideas change the way we see the world.

Different knowledge produces different outcomes. As medi-cal students learn about the body, their eyes are opened to bodi-ly functions they were never able to see before. As a result, they are able to help people when something goes wrong with their bodies. Trained car mechanics have their eyes opened to the principles that make automobiles work—when something goes wrong, they can figure out why. People well versed in socioeco-nomics are able to explain market fluctuations and tell how cer-tain policies are going to affect the country.

When we choose to "eat" from the tree of life, we are choos-ing a certain mentality, an attitude, a way of living. We are choosing to live by the life that God offers all of us through Jesus, His Son. This was the life Jesus talked about constantly and the life that He Himself was:

In him was life, and that life was the light of men (John 1:4).

I [Jesus] have come that they may have life, and have it to the full (John 10:10).

I [Jesus] am the resurrection and the life (John 11:25).

I [Jesus] am the way and the truth and the life (John 14:6).

THE TREE OF LIFE IS A PICTURE OF WALKING AND TALKING WITH GOD— LIVING IN HIS PROVISION, PROTECTION, FELLOWSHIP, FRIENDSHIP AND LORDSHIP.

The tree of life is a picture of walking and talking with God—living in His provision, protection, fellowship, friendship and lordship. It's a picture of living life full of His Spirit, resting in Him and having a clean conscience. It's innocence. But innocence is quickly destroyed when we choose the forbidden—the tree of the knowledge of good and evil. When we choose this tree, although it is appealing to all of us, it brings a completely different outlook—an outlook of death.

George Washington Carver, one of our greatest American heroes, exemplified living in the tree of life. Because he was the son of slave parents and raised in abject poverty, he had valid reasons to be bitter and angry. But he chose not to let the knowledge of good and evil infect his spirit and poison his heart and life. He said, "I will never let another man ruin my life by making me hate him." Consequently, his brilliant mind was not limited by a bitter spirit, which released him to become one of the greatest inventors in American history.

Jesus could have been poisoned by the injustices of his day, and he could have died spiritually. But he consumed the tree of life Himself, and it made all the difference.

Tree-of-Life Innocence

> Let the little children come to me, and do not hinder them, for the kingdom of heaven belongs to such as these (Matt. 19:14).

Gayle and I have perfect children (as you might imagine), four of whom are boys. On more than one occasion, Gayle and I have been sitting in our living room with friends while our three youngest boys were supposed to be taking baths, only to have them come running down the stairs completely naked. Everyone always laughs as they dash through the house with their uncovered little bodies being hotly pursued by their embarrassed mother. It's all right because it's innocent. They're children.

On the other hand, sometimes I notice that my children shield their hearts from me. They hide. When that happens, I seek them out and try to get them to talk to me. Usually something has happened to place a barrier between them and me. It's my responsibility as their father to coach them in living honorable lives so that shame never boxes them into isolation from others.

I believe that's why God came looking for Adam and Eve after they sinned against Him (see Gen. 3:8,9). He knew they had filled themselves with the knowledge of good and evil in an attempt to be more like Him. They had pursued Him according to what appeared to be good, pleasing and desirable. Their pursuit didn't appear to be bad, painful or repulsive, but it was.

And the serpent had been right—their eyes were indeed opened and they realized they were naked. They had always been naked, of course, but it had never been an issue before. Now, with the knowledge of good and evil in their lives, it became a point of shame. Genesis 3:7 says "they realized they were naked; so they sewed fig leaves together and made coverings for themselves." They were ashamed of themselves and wanted to cover up. Their innocence was gone.

When God saw Adam and Eve, He asked, "Who told you that you were naked?" (Gen. 3:11). God had not even wanted them to know. He wanted them to maintain innocence, freely enjoying Him, His creation and one another. But the knowledge of good and evil gives us a value system that tells us we are naked and should hide from God. It stifles innocence and makes us work to cover ourselves.

Many times when I see people come to Christ, they have a sinless look on their faces that communicates childlike innocence. They look clean. Through the years I've noticed that believers who understand living in the tree of life have this same childlike purity about them. I'm convinced that innocence is the by-product of knowing Jesus, and it is the conduit for His anointing.

Men like Billy Graham, T. L. Osborn and John Arnott from Toronto are great examples of the strength of innocence. They have remained untainted throughout years of ministry, which actually disturbs their critics. They respond to criticism with simple honesty, preventing it from hardening their hearts and ruining the anointing.

Women such as Ruth Graham, Freda Lindsey and the late Katherine Kuhlman have responded the same way. Even though they are aware of their shortcomings, they have stayed above the seductions of the knowledge of good and evil and have remained free to minister His freedom. Throughout the years, all of these people have maintained a simple childlikeness that allows the Holy Spirit to freely flow through them. God likes that. Like children, they have more fun than most, and that's refreshing.

Victimization

How do we respond, then, when things go wrong? Do we blame God, ourselves or others? In Adam's case, he blamed Eve and God. "The woman you put here with me," he complained to God, "she gave me some fruit from the tree, and I ate it" (Gen. 3:12).

Eve also quickly learned how to place blame—"The serpent deceived me, and I ate," she said (v. 13).

Here we see another evidence that death entered their hearts. They were blaming each other. When we live according to the tree of the knowledge of good and evil, the double-edged sword of victimization begins its attack. One edge of the sword cuts us. Sometimes it convinces us that we can't obey God, because someone else's actions or our personal weaknesses prevent us. Adam blamed Eve; Eve blamed the snake; their son Cain blamed Abel—and they all created a legacy that we continue to follow.

But displacing responsibility never helps. As soon as we place blame, we are saying that Jesus is not really our Lord—whoever or whatever "made us do it" is.

Some people will actually try to do something to offend you to gain control of your life. They know they'll win some kind of influence over you if you have to rant and rave about something they've done. But if you respond with tree-of-life innocence, they can't get to you. You've maintained your freedom.

The other side of the sword of victimization cuts the people around us. This side of the blade is rooted in pride. If I believe it is godly to read five chapters of the Bible a day, and I successfully read those five chapters, then I'm establishing my own standard for godliness. My knowledge of good and evil tells me that when I read my five chapters, God likes me and I am secure in Him. When I meet other people who also read their five chapters, then they meet my standard, and I can accept them. But when I meet Christians who are not reading five chapters, I start thinking that something is wrong with them. "Don't they know they need to read five chapters a day to be godly?!"

Victimization produces guilt and insists upon punishment. It provides fertile soil for the serpent to accuse and condemn. It always uses fear, and it causes people to focus on the past and dread the future. It finds fault, places blame and demands retribution whenever possible. Victimization loves darkness and entices us to hide portions of our lives, to cover over failure and to avoid accepting responsibility.

Because victimization uses guilt, it prompts us to make promises and vows that can't be kept and will soon be broken, and to develop powerless ideals that cannot be fulfilled. Then a sense of failure begins to define the way we view ourselves and our relationship with God and others, causing us to lose the joy and peace that Christ intended for us to have through His blood sacrifice on the cross.

Living in the tree of life is the opposite of victimization. When we live in the tree of life, we are virtually beyond offense. Jesus, the model of tree-of-life living, put this succinctly in the Sermon on the Mount recorded in Matthew 5: "If someone strikes you on the right cheek, turn to him the other also," He said. "And if someone wants to sue you and take your tunic, let him have your cloak as well. If someone forces you to go one mile, go with him two miles. Give to the one who asks you, and do not turn away from the one who wants to borrow from you" (Matt. 5:39-42). This is not doormat behavior—it is innocent living. It's a tree-of-life attitude.

Responding to Sin with Life

He [God] has made us competent as ministers of a new covenant—not of the letter but of the Spirit; for the letter kills, but the Spirit gives life (2 Cor. 3:6).

Two women can stand outside an abortion clinic and hold signs that read "Stop Abortion Now." Even though they are dressed the same and protest the same problem in the same way, one may be living in the tree of life and the other in the knowledge of good and evil. The difference is the motivation of their hearts.

The tree-of-life protester is there because of her love for the unborn and compassion for the mother and father. She wants to try to help those who are struggling with their pregnancies and help them know they have better options than abortion. The tree-of-the-knowledge-of-good-and-evil protestor is there because abortion is evil, those who participate in it are evil and they must be stopped. These subtle differences in motivation make all the difference in the world.

One way we can tell which tree we are living in is our response to sin. Our response to our own sin can only be adequately settled through Christ; but one of the greatest marks of bearing His character is our response to someone else's sin. If we handle others' mistakes with a life-giving attitude, then we (and they) have the opportunity to enjoy great power and freedom. But if we handle others' mistakes negatively, then we're eating from the wrong tree and will begin to die.

The serpent still asks, "Did God really say . . . ?" and continues to offer many things that draw people away from the life Christ offers. For some, the enticement is a religious life—being "good." For others, it's good works in the secular world. For others, it's blatant evil. Satan doesn't care as long as people miss out on Christ's empowering life. Then he has accomplished his task of keeping people in darkness so they will spend eternity in hell. Jesus, however, wants people to come to Him and to receive life and have the knowledge that His life is the only way we can live in freedom forever.

Living innocently in the tree of life does not mean rejecting the idea of good and evil. In Genesis 4, God clearly explains to Cain that if he will do the right thing, he will be accepted. God is not saying that right actions are the same as living in the life of God; He is saying there is a path of life. The people on that path grow in their understanding of right and wrong, and they find great insight, wisdom, victory and joy in the stream of Jesus' righteousness. These people have a high view of right and wrong and use it to direct themselves and others toward life. Some people, though, base their understanding of right and wrong in the wrong tree. The results are frustration, judgmental attitudes and death.

Religion or Relationship?

I love to travel all over the world and take teams with me to teach the Bible and pray for the outpouring of the Holy Spirit. On these journeys, we have visited the mosques, temples, churches and religious sites of every major religion, where I find sincere people searching for God. Most of these worshipers pray, read holy books, burn candles, rub beads, give offerings, dip in rivers and pour water over statues in their deep pursuit of a relationship with the Almighty God. Few actually find Him, but they don't realize it because they experience a sense of spiritual fulfillment through the soulish satisfaction that comes from the tree of the knowledge of good and evil.

Most religious people know they have had a spiritual experience because it has enlightened them. And, as with Eve, their spiritual devotion (at least temporarily) produces a positive change in their lives—it is good for food and pleasing to the eye.

Unfortunately, these characteristics are universal in all religions, including Christianity. Many "Christians," practicing Jews, Islamic worshipers, Hindus and Buddhists all enjoy the benefits of the knowledge of good and evil. Only those who have pressed through religious practice and have truly come to know the God of Abraham, Isaac and Jacob through His Son, Jesus, can know God. For it is in knowing Him that the mystery of genuine godliness starts to unfold. And it is, indeed, a relationship that is a narrow path—a path that can only be navigated according to the Scriptures by the Holy Spirit. It's easy, but it requires the understanding of relationship, not just knowledge of a creed. That is why, after Genesis 3, we start to see story after story of God's encounters with people as He teaches them about Himself. He's a person and we are His people; and to have His life we must learn to know Him.

In Galatians 5, the apostle Paul lists the acts of the sinful nature and the fruit of the Spirit. Many people who study these lists think of them as evil things to avoid and good things to do. Not so. Each list is a mirror that helps us to see if we are living a Spirit-filled life. The message is to discover the truth of the gospel and to be increasingly filled with the Holy Spirit so that genuine freedom in Christ can be found.

That's why the Bible doesn't simply give us an arbitrary creed to live by. It's more personal than that. Jesus told the scribes and the Pharisees, "You diligently study the Scriptures because you think that by them you possess eternal life. *These are the Scriptures that testify about me, yet you refuse to come to me to have life*" (John 5:39,40, italics added).

These good people studied the Scriptures diligently and missed the point completely, just as we so often do. They were neither studying the Scriptures nor living their lives in the tree of life, but were studying and living according to the tree of the knowledge of good and evil. That's why Jesus called them white-washed tombs and vipers (see Matt. 23:27,33). Jesus rebuked the biblical scholars of His day for missing the primary messages of the Scriptures, but He loved the humble worshipers who had childlike hearts. He said:

> I praise you, Father, Lord of heaven and earth, because you have hidden these things from the wise and learned, and revealed them to little children. Yes, Father, for this was your good pleasure (Matt. 11:25,26).

It is important to understand that Jesus was not speaking against thoughtful understanding of the Scriptures. Nor should we construe that God's warning about the knowledge of good and evil could be an exhortation to keep us from studying and gaining knowledge. He was simply emphasizing the necessity of a heart submitted and open to Him. We don't just read the Word and believe it—we become it through knowing Him.

Jesus knew that His teaching had to help people transition from the tree of the knowledge of good and evil to the tree of life.

Because much of Judaism had become a religion of "godly" action instead of a relationship with God, Jesus had to challenge the fundamental way the Scriptures were being applied. So He emphasized that without a relationship with Him, a relationship with the Father was impossible. That's why He said to eat His body and drink His blood. Christianity is much more than an intellectual assent to the principles of the Bible; it requires actually consuming Him so that His life dominates our lives.

Staying in the Tree of Life

Sometimes we jump between the two trees like monkeys swinging from limb to limb. We can be living joyfully in the tree of life one moment, only to have someone say something critical that causes us to jump into the tree of the knowledge of good and evil and become sinfully defensive. Often when we hear criticism, we can feel the clouds forming in our hearts, warning us that we're about to fight back. But we like the fight, so we give in. It feels good to prove to someone how you are right and they are wrong. But even when we are technically right, we are achieving an empty victory at best. In other words, we are right—*dead* right!

Now I've learned that I can remain in the tree of life even when I'm criticized. An innocent response leaves my heart clean and gives my critic a better opportunity to find the tree of life as well. With tree-of-life living, I can respond and explain myself, but everyone stays clean. That's genuine victory.

When we go to church in the tree of life, we are grateful for the congregation, grateful for the staff and grateful for the leadership. We want to make ourselves available to serve. It's a joy to give, a delight to worship and easy to pray and fellowship with those around us. But attending church in the tree of the knowledge of good and evil is quite different. We go because of duty or obligation, not because we draw life from church. When we get there, we attend with a critical eye. If the pastor, the volume of the sound system, the temperature or the music isn't quite right, a sour spirit starts developing in our hearts. And if a need surfaces somewhere in the church, rather than manifesting a compassionate desire to help, we criticize.

Bible reading can have the same dynamic. When I read the Bible from the tree-of-life perspective, joy is always a part of my reading. Like a child, I submit to the Scriptures and let them speak deeply into my heart. I can always tell when I'm in the tree of life because I want to mark lots of the verses and make prolific notes. But I've had other times when I've read my Bible from the knowledge-of-good-and-evil point of view, and it becomes a tired obligation. The struggle of trying to get through a certain number of chapters or trying to read for a certain time period every day can be a source of death.

When I was in high school, I read a chapter from the Bible every night before I went to sleep, no matter how late the hour or how tired I was. At the time, that was a real blessing to me. Since then I have set other goals that didn't add fresh life to my spirit but burdened it. So I choose to stay in the tree of life when reading my Bible—my goal in reading it is to know God. If that's my intention, then reading it comes easily to me.

Prayer is the same way. Tree-of-life praying is when worship, intimacy, communion with the Father and an easy connection with the Spirit is natural. Tree-of-life praying is getting into your prayer closet and praying until you're done. Tree-of-the-knowledge-of-good-and-evil praying is different. When you pray only because you think you ought to do it, it becomes a miserable trap. It's dry, rote and lacks connection. It can be satisfying to a degree, but only because it makes us feel as if we've done something good. That is not nearly as satisfying as knowing His life.

In the tree of the knowledge of good and evil, we mistakenly believe that doing good is an end in itself. It's good to go to church, to protest abortion, to pray and read our Bibles. It's good to be good. It's better to be good than evil. But goodness is not *life* unless it is a result of His life.

The tree of the knowledge of good and evil is a legalistic, self-righteous mind-set. We know what is right and wrong when we are in the tree of life, but our attitude and expression of right and wrong are on a different level.

Of course, living in the tree of life does include constructive discipline. When I pray, I ask God to convict me strongly so I can live in the refreshment of His Spirit. That conviction keeps me clean, and His discipline motivates me to live well. It bears emphasizing: Both good and bad people are dead without life. Life comes from Christ alone, and His fruit is righteousness. So righteousness motivated in the knowledge of good and evil is empty; but righteousness birthed in the life of God gives us the ability to be life-giving ourselves; thus we are able to build life-giving churches full of joy and power—churches that rest in Him.

RELATIONSHIPS THAT EMPOWER

Two are better than one, because they have a good return for their work: if one falls down, his friend can help him up. But pity the man who falls and has no one to help him up! Also, if two lie down together, they will keep warm. But how can one keep warm alone? Though one may be overpowered, two can defend themselves. A cord of three strands is not quickly broken.

E C C L E S I A S T E S   4 : 9 - 1 2

THE DIVINE FLOW OF RELATIONSHIPS

Moses and Aaron needed one another. Moses had been commissioned by God to speak to Pharaoh, the most powerful man in the world, and to demand that Pharaoh let God's people go. But Moses stuttered. Aaron was the articulate one. So when Aaron joined Moses, Moses was able to do more than he could have done alone.

Aaron was commissioned by God to lead the people of Israel while Moses was away. Aaron was in the correct position to lead, but he lacked confidence and faith, and he was easily pressured by people. But when Moses joined Aaron, Aaron was empowered to do more than he could have done alone.

Every individual needs to be connected to others in order to do what God wants him or her to do. God made us this way. He made us in such a way that we need each other's help. God Himself is One, but He is also three persons in relationship with one another. The Father sent the Son; the Son sent the Holy Spirit; and the Holy Spirit brings glory to the Father through the Son. Three persons, but one God.

God has given us natural relationships that reflect His three-in-one dynamic. Marriage, our families, the church, a community, friendships and alliances—all are opportunities for us to relate to and strengthen one another. People are weak when they don't know how to connect with others. But with connection, great tasks can be accomplished.

Not only do relationships empower people, but they also empower ministry. Sometimes we make the mistake of thinking that position empowers ministry; that is, we think that if only we had a certain position we would be able to do better ministry. Positions are important, but they are not ministry. Positions give us chain of command in our organizations and our job descriptions, but they don't give us ministry. Ministry comes exclusively from a series of empowering relationships.

"Relationships are the only thing we take to heaven with us," an old Baptist preacher once said. I've heard businesspeople say that everything they know is subordinated to their people skills. If they cannot relate well with people, then their ability to provide goods and services to others is greatly hampered. A board member of one of the world's largest corporations told me that people who understand relationships are the ones who enjoy true success.

Some people grumble that success is too often based on who we know rather than what we know. That may make us uncomfortable, but it's true. Relationships are everything. Even our eternal destinies are determined by our personal relationship with Jesus Christ. If we know Him, we go to heaven; if we don't know Him, we do not.

Several years ago I read a little booklet by John Osteen, a pastor in Houston, Texas, entitled *The Divine Flow*. This booklet explains how the Holy Spirit creates a divine flow between people's hearts that, if responded to properly, can supernaturally build relationship. Sometimes this divine flow feels like a welling up of love or a desire to devote special attention toward a particular person. Other times the divine flow causes us to have an unusual interest in another person.

Pastor Osteen develops the idea further by applying it to our relationships within the Church. He explains that we can often determine God's perfect plan in building purposeful relationships for His kingdom by learning to respond to the divine flow in our hearts. He says we should learn to sense God's divine flow toward other people because it may mean we are supposed to work together in a meaningful way in His kingdom.

Several years ago I was asked to speak to the Godly Men Conference at Oral Roberts University. During the meeting, I noticed a divine flow in my heart toward the worship leader, Ross Parsley, who is now a trusted friend and the worship pastor here at New Life. In that same series of meetings, a student working in the lobby of the chapel, Russ Walker, caught my attention. Because of this connection, several years later he became the associate pastor who helped to implement free-market small groups in our church.

LIFE-GIVING

MINISTRY FLOWS

THROUGH GODLY

RELATIONSHIPS,

NOT JUST

CORPORATE

STRUCTURES.

The flow can happen both ways. Another student who attended the conference, John Bolin, had a miracle happen in his heart that touched his spirit. He felt a sense of being connected with me, even though we hadn't met. Now, years later, he and his wife, Sarah, have moved to Colorado Springs and serve on our senior leadership team. Joseph Thompson, another friend, read my book *Primary Purpose* and experienced a powerful sense of connectedness with me. As a result, he and his family are now here, basing their ministry out of our church.

Life-giving ministry flows through godly relationships, not just corporate structures. It is relationships with family members, elders, staff members, community leaders, the press and volunteers that are the core of life-giving ministries. When God creates supernatural relationships to make us more effective—if they are honorably maintained—they can empower and enable us to fulfill God's calling.

There are seven sets of relationships that empower successful life-giving ministry. All of these relationships funnel people toward eternal life through Christ; the more levels we understand, the more effective our ministries can become. As you read the list, notice that each additional level of relationship has increased breadth of impact, and each level requires its own revelation or unique understanding on our part. These relationships are the way God strengthens us to fulfill His calling. He wants us to understand and flow in relationships that empower us to do what He wants done.

Relationship #1: Jesus

Result: Salvation

> If anyone would come after me, he must deny himself and take up his cross daily and follow me. For whoever wants to save his life will lose it, but whoever loses his life for me will save it (Luke 9:23,24).

Jesus is the cornerstone of the Church. Our relationship with Him is foundational to every other relationship and empowers us to assist others. Once our relationship with Him is secure and growing, then He is able to create and maintain all of our other relationships, which will lead to healthy ministry. He is the life-giver for all life-giving relationships. He is the foundation of every life-giving church.

In order to have a life-giving ministry, we must be confident that we have been born again into a vital relationship with Christ. In this generation of "easy-believism," many people think they have been born again when, in fact, they have not. Jesus said,

> Not everyone who says to me, "Lord, Lord," will enter the kingdom of heaven, but only he who does the will of my

Father who is in heaven. Many will say to me on that day, "Lord, Lord, did we not prophesy in your name, and in your name drive out demons and perform many miracles?" Then I will tell them plainly, "I never knew you. Away from me, you evildoers!" (Matt. 7:21-23).

Titus 1:16 drives the point home: "They claim to know God, but by their actions they deny him."

When Jesus gave us the Great Commission to reach the world, He said, "Go and make disciples of all nations, baptizing them in the name of the Father and of the Son and of the Holy Spirit, and teaching them to obey everything I have commanded you" (Matt. 28:19,20). Almost all Christians can quote this, but when they do, they are actually thinking, *Go into all the world and have them recite a prayer.*

Because many people misread the Great Commission, millions of people believe they are born again, but they neither know Him nor live lives that have been transformed by the power of the Holy Spirit (see 2 Cor. 5:17). Philippians 2:12 says, "Continue to work out your salvation with fear and trembling, for it is God who works in you to will and to act according to his good purpose."

Prayer—expressing our heart's repentance—is without a doubt the way we are all born again. But being born again is only the doorway to the ultimate purpose of knowing Him. If we guarantee people that they have begun a relationship with Christ and have received eternal life just because they repeated a prayer, we might be assuming too much. There is no way for any of us to know the condition of another person's heart. So when repeating or reading a prayer, some do begin their relationship with Christ, but others don't. The horrific reality might be that if they were just repeating words and we tell them they are now guaranteed eternal life, we might be giving them false assurance that could contribute to their going to hell. We as life-givers point the way and direct people to Christ; but each individual must faithfully pursue his or her own relationship with Christ and work out his or her own salvation with fear and trembling.

In 1972, when I prayed to receive Christ along with thousands of other high school students at Explo '72, I expressed my love for Christ and my desire to have Him live in me. Upon returning home, I started going to church and reading my Bible, but my internal life did not change. I didn't stop any of my normal non-Christian high school student activities. I was fully living in the world but involved in church and in reading my Bible. Then, after my senior year of high school, my pastor led me in a prayer to "sell out," to commit my entire life to Christ. After that prayer, my life dramatically changed—evidence of becoming a new creation.

So, when did I become a Christian? I tell people I got saved at Explo '72; but something makes me wonder if Explo '72 didn't begin a process that led to a genuine conversion experience two years later. I don't know with assurance, and I don't want to endlessly discuss the salvation process here. But I do want to emphasize that in order to have life-giving churches, we need to know, with absolute assurance and evidence in our hearts and lifestyles, that we are securely and verifiably in a dynamic relationship with Christ.

Relationship #2: Self

Result: Sanctification

May God himself, the God of peace, sanctify you through and through. May your whole spirit, soul and body be

kept blameless at the coming of our Lord Jesus Christ
(1 Thess. 5:23).

Every growing Christian has experienced the war that can sometimes develop between our spirits, our souls (sometimes defined
as our mind, will and emotions) and our bodies. When we come
to Christ, we become new creations spiritually, but our souls and
our bodies are just as they were before conversion. Over time, we
can progress in our growth and get our internal conflicts settled
so we can safely minister to others.

Certain lifestyles portray Christian maturity and give our
witness credibility; other lifestyles do not. That's why the Bible
lists qualifications for eldership and standards for Christian
leaders. Personal sanctification validates His message. If we
attempt to minister without internalizing His life to some
degree, we can horribly embarrass the Body of Christ.

First Thessalonians addresses this issue directly:

It is God's will that you should be sanctified: that you
should avoid sexual immorality; that each of you should
learn to control his own body in a way that is holy and
honorable, not in passionate lust like the heathen, who
do not know God; and that in this matter no one should
wrong his brother or take advantage of him. The Lord
will punish men for all such sins, as we have already told
you and warned you. For God did not call us to be
impure, but to live a holy life (4:3-7).

Sanctification is a process. Time, trial and error, failing and
trying again, thinking, praying, talking and sharing with others
in the Body works sanctification into our lives. Fortunately, God
has given us tools to use along the way and help with the process.

Tool #1: The Word of God—the Bible

Jesus emphasized the role of the Word in the process of sanctification in His John 17:17 prayer: "Sanctify them by the truth; your word is truth." Second Timothy 3:16,17 says, "All Scripture is God-breathed and is useful for teaching, rebuking, correcting and training in righteousness, so that the man of God may be thoroughly equipped for every good work." This verse highlights the importance of the Bible for *teaching*—the Bible gives us information we didn't have, which we can then share with others; *rebuking*—in revealing what is negative, inappropriate or sinful in our lives, the Bible gives strong warnings not to repeat past mistakes; *correcting*—reading Scripture can influence our everyday actions by helping us to adjust to the right or left and keep on His perfect path; and *training*—reading the Bible helps prepare us for the future.

Hebrews 4:12 emphasizes the intrinsic power of God's Word when it says, "For the word of God is living and active. Sharper than any double-edged sword, it penetrates even to dividing soul and spirit, joints and marrow; it judges the thoughts and attitudes of the heart."

I believe that as we read the Bible, we must pray through the ideas on the page. When we study the Bible, we pick up on most of the ideas that the Lord breathed into the heart and mind of the Bible author. Often, though, we can't apply these ideas successfully because we are just reading with our minds, not with our hearts. Then, when we pray through the ideas from the Word of God, God breathes again into our hearts so that we can not only read and believe the principles of the Word of God, but we can actually *become* the principles of the Word.

Christianity is powerful not just because of what we believe, but because of what we become. When we pray God's Word and God breathes into us, He is rewriting His Word on our hearts, thereby sanctifying our lives.

Tool #2: The Spirit of God

Peter emphasized the sanctifying role of the Spirit when he said that we have been chosen "according to the foreknowledge of God the Father, through the sanctifying work of the Spirit, for obedience to Jesus Christ and sprinkling by his blood: Grace and peace be yours in abundance" (1 Pet. 1:2).

The greatest tool I know to stimulate the sanctifying work of the Holy Spirit is prayer and fasting. Three-day fasts with Bible videos and audiocassettes are great opportunities to soak in the Word of God. I encourage people to fast in quiet places where they can rest, sleep and pray, such as hotel rooms or cabins. In this environment, not only does the mind clear and the spirit refresh, but the body also rests and is cleansed.

I think Christian leaders should pray and fast through boredom. When ministry becomes predictable, ordinary or unexciting, prayer and fasting can be a wonderful tool of refreshing. For me, regular three-day fasts are the key to staying fresh and interested. When we do this once a season (summer, fall, winter and spring), we gain perspective, inspiration, strength and spiritual authority. These special times allow us to forgive everyone and/or anything that has hurt, disappointed or betrayed us. It's also an exceptional time to do personal spiritual warfare to ensure that our lives are pure and clean and ready for aggressive growth.

In order to be successful, leave your cell phone, laptop computer and office work at home. Let this be a time with God and nature—no one and nothing else. You need this time. You'll live longer and better; and your spirit will be refreshed and your management of time become more efficient. The Spirit of God will work deeply in you to sanctify your life and body.

Immorality, pride, materialism and hyperindividualism are wreaking havoc in our churches and families. Prayer and fasting are the best way to challenge these cancers in the Body. The basic need that drives so many of these sins is the same basic drive that wants food when you get hungry on your fast. So, if we learn discipline and control over Big Macs, pizza and Mountain Dew, we can apply that discipline to cyber-sex, arrogance, gluttony and greed. We have a choice: We can either learn integrity publicly and potentially embarrass our families and our church, or we can learn integrity alone on a mountain somewhere while praying and fasting.

Tool #3: Committed Relationships

In explaining how God's righteousness is integrated into every area of our lives, the book of Hebrews emphasizes the role of the relationships within the Body of Christ (see 10:19-39). Within the heart of this discussion, Hebrews 10:25 says, "Let us not give up meeting together, as some are in the habit of doing, but let us encourage one another—and all the more as you see the Day approaching." The point is clear: We need relationships with others as part of the sanctification process.

Forging good relationships in marriage, with children, in churches and in other committed relationships serves as a constraint on the darkest sides of us and encourages the development of wisdom. Families, churches and communities work successfully only when people lay aside selfishness and develop goodness. In other words, relationships help to sanctify us.

Tool #4: The Blood of Christ

Hebrews 10:29 talks about the "blood of the covenant" that sanctifies. Without a doubt, the application of the blood of Christ to our lives is vitally important. It is the application of the blood that makes our Christian lives possible in the first place. In Hebrews 9:14 the Bible says, "How much more, then, will the blood of Christ, who through the eternal Spirit offered himself unblemished to God, cleanse our consciences from acts that lead to death, so that we may serve the living God!" There it is with perfect clarity—if we want to serve God, our conscience has to be cleansed by the blood of Jesus.

I love this portion of Scripture because it articulates so well the necessity of the blood and the innocence and childlikeness that results from its work. How is the blood applied? Through repentance—by turning around and changing direction. By submission to God's plan for our lives. The blood sets our lives apart for His service.

Tool #5: A Focused Direction

Making wise daily decisions is extremely important in the work of sanctification. We need to know where we are headed; every choice we make needs to move us in the right direction. Very often Christians fail to recognize the importance of a strong decision for Christ. We have a responsibility to read God's Word and make wise decisions that will line up our lives with God's plans. The Bible commands us to be holy and says that we need to sanctify ourselves. What does that mean? It means that we need to choose not to live an ungodly life, that we need to decide not to pollute our minds, bodies or spirits, and that we need to choose to grow spiritually. Good decisions sanctify us.

Relationship #3: Your Family

Result: Wisdom

> He [an overseer] must manage his own family well and see that his children obey him with proper respect. (If anyone

does not know how to manage his own family, how can he take care of God's church?) (1 Tim. 3:4,5).

With the traditional family model under siege by Western culture, it's more important than ever that we preserve close family dynamics within the Christian community. The home is the primary place God has designed as training to create positive, healthy relationships.

Every relational dynamic we need to know to build a life-giving church can be developed within the school of the home. Paul says in Ephesians 5:22-33 that the relationship between the husband and the wife is to model the relationship that exists between Christ and the Church. A loving husband-and-wife relationship provides insight into God's love for His people, the dynamic of servant-style leadership, the qualities of mutual love, compassion, nurturance, intimacy, respect and generosity.

Gayle and I have five children. Before our children came along, I thought the role of parents was to help their children grow up. I have since discovered this is only partially true. Children help their parents grow up, too. You can't be childish and be successful at rearing children. Children teach us how to live for others and how to relate to various ages. Babies do not care about income, titles or influence. They demand our attention and respect. If we withhold it, they punish us. Adolescents give us constant opportunities to learn how to train and teach. A teenager's behavior fluctuates on a daily basis—you have to learn to ride the roller coaster with them and stay steady.

Children in relationship with siblings learn important lessons, too. In our home, Christy is 19, Marcus is 17, Jonathan is 13, Alex is 10 and Elliott is 8. When any of them fight, they must settle their differences. No one can leave home while fighting. "Divorces" are not allowed—we all have to adjust to and understand one another. And we have to know who is in charge. If any of us becomes selfish, the home becomes unhappy for everyone. If a job needs to be done, it is accomplished with greatest ease when we all work together.

The principles learned in the home are not only transferrable but are essential for successfully leading a healthy church. Just as the home has rules of decency, kindness, respect, honor and contentment, these qualities are also necessary for a life-giving church. The balance of law and grace, autocratic rule and group dynamics, meting out justice and discipline are ideas we all must learn in order to have a both a healthy home and a life-giving church.

Relationship #4: The Small Group

Result: Function

> As iron sharpens iron, so one man sharpens another (Prov. 27:17).

Every successful church has some method for helping people form dynamic friendships within the Body. Some churches use cell groups or small group systems to accomplish this goal, while others use Sunday School classes. Regardless of the form used to cultivate closeness, every successful pastor knows that friendships within the Body are what hold the church together and cause it to function.

Any demon, no matter how weak, can penetrate a corporate structure. But no demon, no matter how strong, can penetrate a genuine friendship. At New Life, hundreds of small groups meet every week. Because of those groups, new friendships are constantly forming, which helps our church family to stay strong and healthy.

Many of the great Bible heroes understood genuine friendship. In the book of Ruth, Naomi is told by Ruth, "Don't urge me to leave you or to turn back from you. Where you go I will go, and where you stay I will stay. Your people will be my people and your God my God" (1:16). First Samuel 20:17 is one of many verses that talk about the way David and Jonathan strengthened one another: "Jonathan had David reaffirm his oath out of love for him, because he loved him as he loved himself."

The Gospels make note of several of the friendships Jesus maintained. Some people just wanted to serve the Lord, while others were His disciples. Matthew 27:55 says, "Many women were there, watching from a distance. They had followed Jesus from Galilee to care for his needs." In the Garden of Gethsemane, Jesus wanted His closest friends—Peter, James and John—with Him. He drew strength from His friends, just as we do (see Matt. 26:36-46).

Strong, healthy friendships make all of us feel more secure, positive in attitude, and productive and effective in what we do than we ever could alone. Friendships produce an upward synergy that activates strength. Paul was very frank about his relationships with the Church at Philippi when he wrote:

I thank my God every time I remember you. In all my prayers for all of you, I always pray with joy because of your partnership in the gospel from the first day until now. It is right for me to feel this way about all of you, since I have you in my heart; . . . God can testify how I long for all of you with the affection of Christ Jesus. And this is my prayer: that your love may abound more and more in knowledge and depth of insight (Phil. 1:3-5,7-9).

SMALL GROUPS

KEEP THE

LOCAL CHURCH

FUNCTIONING AS

A LIFE-GIVING

BODY LINKED

TOGETHER WITH

THE SINEW

OF POSITIVE

RELATIONSHIPS.

Paul understood the importance of the divine flow in genuine friendships that teach us how to function within the calling God has given us. We too can experience this type of friendship within small groups, which refine the righteousness God is working into our lives in practical ways. Small groups teach us how to apply the lessons we have learned in our walk with Christ to our family relationships and our public lives. Honest friendships keep us from being deceived or becoming hypocritical. I can attest that my friends sharpen me and help me to see my blind spots.

I would go so far as to say that small groups are the strength of the local church. They keep it from evolving into a simple religious organization and keep it functioning as a life-giving body linked together with the sinew of positive relationships.

Relationship #5: The Local Church

Result: Interdependence

It was he who gave some to be apostles, some to be prophets, some to be evangelists, and some to be pastors and teachers, to prepare God's people for works of service, so that the body of Christ may be built up until we all reach unity in the faith and in the knowledge of the Son of God and become mature, attaining to the whole measure of the fullness of Christ. From him the whole body, joined and held together by every supporting ligament, grows and builds itself up in love, as each part does its work (Eph. 4:11-13,16).

In 1 Corinthians 12, the Bible reminds us that we are a body with many members, which only functions when all parts are working together. When we worship, give, learn and grow together as a local church, our cumulative impact dramatically increases. In local churches, our unified prayer, financial strength and mutual encouragement cause us to form a body of Christians capable of accomplishing tasks that would be impossible in smaller groups.

Our local churches are God's storehouses of dynamic power for learning to function in the strength of interdependence. Ephesians 4:16 emphasizes the role of interdependent relationships within the local church when it talks about the Body being "joined and held together by every supporting ligament." Those supporting ligaments are the healthy relationships within the Body that cause it to grow, to build itself up and to work. God's plan for His people cannot be fulfilled unless we gather as a local church so the apostles, prophets, evangelists, pastors and teachers can equip us to effectively work in His kingdom.

Relationship #6: The City Church

Result: Momentum

To the angel of the church in Ephesus, Smyrna, Pergamum, Thyatira, Sardis, Philadelphia and Laodicea write (see Rev. 2:1,8,12,18; 3:1,7,14).

All around the world the Holy Spirit is speaking to the Body about forming citywide coalitions of local churches to promote evangelism. These coalitions are groups of churches that strengthen one another by forming strategic alliances. The coalition of churches in Colorado Springs has three goals:

1. We pray for every person in our city by name at least once a year.
2. We communicate the gospel, in an understandable way, to every person in our city at least once a year.
3. We want an additional 1 percent of our city's population to attend church each weekend by the end of each year. For our city, that means an additional 5,000 people saved and discipled in our churches citywide every year.

Several networks of churches coordinate our citywide efforts. Individually, our churches could not have accomplished these goals, but as a group of churches, we can achieve them with relative ease. This network of relationships makes all of our jobs simpler and causes our churches to grow through conversion growth rather than competing for transfer growth.

Just as individual Christians need to connect with others in a healthy local church in order to grow strong, so local churches can connect with other local churches to become increasingly effective. My book *Primary Purpose* discusses "how to make it hard to go to hell from your city." Jack Hayford and I coauthored a book on city strategies entitled *Loving Your City into the Kingdom*. Bill Bright, Peter Wagner, Ed Silvoso, George Otis, Jr., George Barna and others contributed to this book, and it is an excellent resource for all Christians. Another recommended resource for city strategies is Ed Silvoso's book *That None Should Perish*.

Relationship #7: The Global Church

Result: Completion

> After this I looked and there before me was a great mul-
> titude that no one could count, from every nation, tribe,
> people and language, standing before the throne and in
> front of the Lamb. They were wearing white robes and
> were holding palm branches in their hands (Rev. 7:9).

The final set of relationships that empower us for effective ministry is the network of relationships we as local churches form to enable missionary activities. These efforts require local churches to take a portion of their tithes and strategically use the money to ensure that every person living in our generation has an opportunity to hear the gospel. To fulfill this task, we must work in harmony with the other members of the Body of Christ in increasingly broader relationships. By working as members of the family, the small group, the local church, the city church and the global church, we can see Jesus' calling on our lives fulfilled.

As we receive the revelation from His Spirit and the Scriptures about our purpose in His kingdom, it becomes evident that each of these sets of relationships are vital to His purposes and are dependent upon one another. Relationships are not optional for any of us. Productive, empowering relationships make ministry easy, delightful and efficient with maximum breadth of impact. They are foundational to building a life-giving church.

CHAPTER FIVE

THE STAGES OF GROWTH AND CRISIS

God, who has called you into fellowship with his Son
Jesus Christ our Lord, is faithful.
1 CORINTHIANS 1:9

KNOWING WHAT TO EXPECT

I love pastoral work. To me, there is nothing negative about it. Our message is so wonderful, our freedom so real. If we can just implement a structure that gives freedom for spiritual growth and enables people to grow in ministry, everything about a local church can be positive.

Sometimes when I say this, people laugh (while others cry), because so few people enjoy pastoral work. But in my mind, a church is like a family. If you can coach it and disciple it, then everyone's life can become a blessing.

I do love ministry. I love Easter and Christmas celebrations. I love the choir, the children's ministry and the small groups. I love watching people learn to live abundantly. Some pastors, though, struggle with local church ministry because they have never understood how to keep a church healthy year after year. They sometimes have a difficult time gauging the status of their church's health—they don't know how to answer the essential question, How are we doing?

The duties of a pastorate can seem chaotic and unpredictable, but they don't have to be. In reality, there are natural stages of crisis and growth that virtually all churches go through. Recognizing those stages is essential to maintaining a perspective in a steady, life-giving ministry.

Every church should have a pattern of growth and assimilation. If your church stays the same size year after year, there is obviously a problem. But if your church grows by leaps and bounds every year without ever incorporating the new people and making them a vital part of the fellowship, you still have a problem. Every pastor should go through times when his main focus is on getting new people assimilated into the congregation. There will also be times when his main focus is on getting to know the people and caring for the ones who are already there.

Unfortunately, many pastors overreact by mistaking times of assimilation as plateaus. Overreaction is not healthy. It causes undue worry and, ironically, can trigger a downward spiral for an otherwise healthy church. When growth slows down a bit, often the Holy Spirit is giving us opportunities to strengthen the inner workings of our churches, to develop new leaders within the congregation and to open some new small groups.

Healthy annual growth percentages range from 10 to 20 percent. New Life has been in this range for 15 years now, and there are no signs that we'll be experiencing dramatic growth above that range or a sharp decline in the near future (as of this writing, we are 18.2 percent above last year). If you are in that range, you've got a good thing happening. If you go very far above 20 percent growth, you need to be extra alert about assimilation—connecting people with people. I call growth that goes beyond 20 percent "hypergrowth"—it feels good, but it's hard for people to really get to know one another. We are always grateful when God is blessing our church by adding to our numbers, but we also know that we need to pay extra close attention to our small groups, youth programs and so on, and ensure that the new people are becoming part of the Body.

If you fall below the 10 to 20 percent range, you need to find the bottleneck and address the problem creatively. At this growth rate, the church will become stale, you won't have the resources to integrate new personalities and their strengths, and you may even start to decline. You may need to implement a new system of small groups (see chapter 11), funnel more resources into youth ministry, and examine your outreach methods. If you are below zero percent growth, the potential for downward spiral is real. People will start noticing who isn't there anymore. This requires dramatic action—you need to seriously address the fundamental issues, which are leadership, style, and so on.

Again, healthy churches will have times of growth followed by times of assimilation. The growth chart of your church should not shoot straight up. It should look like the graph on page 89.

There are two exceptions to this principle. In C. Peter Wagner's book *The Healthy Church*, he describes two situations that would cause a church to plateau (or decline) almost irrevocably: *ethnikitis* (a dramatic shift in the ethnicity of a community) and *ghost town disease* (a dramatic deterioration in the overall population of a community). Wagner's book deftly teaches how to deal with both of these scenarios with grace and integrity and also shows how to correct other "curable" diseases that may be infecting stagnated or declining churches.

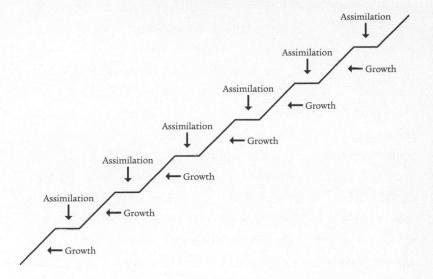

THE STAGES OF GROWTH AND CRISIS

Some time ago, one of the men from our congregation, Dan Brokke, came into my office and gave me a chart he had found in the *Harvard Business Review*. Dan had been using the chart in his leadership training at David C. Cook Ministries, where he was serving at the time. As I looked over the chart with him, which explained how businesses go through a natural progression of growth periods and crises, I realized that the same principles applied to churches, to individual departments in a church and even to individual employees in a church.

Whenever we grow, the growth itself will create a series of crises that, if addressed, will open the door for further growth.

That is, we will grow in a certain way, then have a certain crisis, then—if we respond to that crisis appropriately—grow again and have another type of crisis, and so on. We shouldn't be discouraged when a crisis happens. We should expect these stages to happen and be prepared in advance.

1. Crisis of
LEADERSHIP

1. Growth through
← CREATIVITY

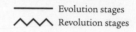

——— Evolution stages
〰〰 Revolution stages

Stage One Growth: Creativity

Creativity is the stage we all love; it is the growth stage when we receive inspiration to plant a church, to come up with fresh ideas or to birth a new ministry within the church with a fresh vision for the future. God plants an idea in our hearts and causes us to see what is unique about what we want to do with our church. For me, this happened over 15 years ago when I was praying and fasting in the mountains of Colorado. At that time, God gave me the vision I described in the first chapter of this book. Everything I have done since then has been a response to that vision.

What makes creativity a stage of growth? When you are inspired to do something, you have already begun to grow. In a sense, you begin to move forward immediately upon capturing the vision. You pray, fast, seek counsel, talk to your friends and family and begin to take practical steps. Burgeoning creativity does not allow you to remain in the same place or stay exactly the same person you were before. You have already been changed. As the idea is birthed in your heart and mind, you automatically begin taking steps toward the completion of that vision.

Creativity is something that should never stop, even when you are many years into the initial vision. At a couple of stages in the growth of New Life, we have creatively reworked some of the foundation of how we function as a church (as you will see more particularly in the chapter on small groups). Each department should periodically revisit creative elements and reshape the way ministry is done. The Holy Spirit is always giving fresh, new ideas, and we must remain ever open to His influence.

At New Life, we ask employees who have been in the church for a while to attend one conference a year to stimulate creativity in their lives. My rule is that no one can apply what he or she has learned in a conference for at least three months. By that time the emotional high has lessened and the best ideas remain. In addition, we ask that all church employees on the leadership team read one book a month and alternate between a Christian book and a secular book every other month. As they do this, they are constantly introduced to new ideas and thoughts that keep them thinking creatively.

Probably the most important discipline to keep a church creative is proactive prayer and fasting. I recommend that people take three days to pray and fast every season—four times a year. But I don't like passive fasting or fasting because of negative situations, even though sometimes this is inevitable. I like staff members to pray and fast in order to soak in God's Word, to rest and to ask God to work in them so they can reach ever higher, run farther, expand their circle of love and wash the feet of more people. That is proactive prayer and fasting. It makes people push forward in optimism and in the power and life of God, rather than getting stuck in excessive introspection that can discourage growth.

Stage One Crisis: Leadership

This first crisis in selecting leadership is an important key to the future growth of your church. In the leadership crisis stage, you begin to establish your key staff members and other leadership. If you don't know how to settle this issue, your church will never effectively grow. If you settle it correctly, you will immediately begin to move into the next stage.

The federal government allows churches up to two years to get their organizational structure in order before they receive their letter of determination from the IRS that recognizes them as a nonprofit organization. Churches often go through this stage too quickly and appoint elders, deacons, trustees and associates before they have fully considered the candidates. When the church is in this growth stage, it needs to carefully form a leadership team of friends who are interested in getting the ministry to people, not people who are overly interested in titles and salaries.

At New Life Church, we have several levels of leadership. Directly above me are the overseers, who would have the authority to fire or discipline me if there were any problems. These people should have been around for years and have proven ministries in a local church (preferably at least three of them should have proven ministries in an apostolic-style church). These overseers must be exceptionally strong and steady, because they will provide stability for the church and open the door for future growth.

The next level of leadership is your team of trustees. This group is the business board of your church. They ensure that the processes of borrowing money, signing leases, buying property or building a facility are well done. This is also the group that signs off on the budget, which gives people increased confidence that the church is here to stay and that everything is well done and in order.

The overseers and trustees do their work somewhat behind the scenes. They are foundational infrastructure. Their presence assures the people that their financial and time investments are secure.

The next level of leadership is the group of associate or assistant pastors, staff and volunteers. This is your team that touches people's lives by answering the phones, working in the nursery, organizing events, planning outreach, leading prayer meetings, and so on. This team should be made up of friends who are predominantly the age of the senior pastor or younger. This is the public team that does the public work.

The final leadership team I'll mention here is the elders. This is a group of men and women in your church who meet the qualifications of eldership and derive their income from secular employment. These men and women are not governing elders; they are ministering elders. Their role is to minister to people and to the church staff and to spiritually protect the staff and serve the congregation.

There are actually three levels of eldership: the overseers, the pastoral team, and the team with whom we actually use the term "elder." We will discuss this last group in chapter 12.

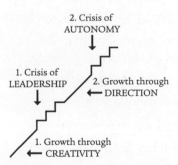

2. Crisis of
AUTONOMY

1. Crisis of
LEADERSHIP

2. Growth through
DIRECTION

1. Growth through
CREATIVITY

Stage Two Growth: Direction

With the excitement of creativity and the security and enthusiasm of fresh leadership, the church will continue to grow through the next phase by clearly articulating and pursuing the questions, Where are we headed? and Where is the church going? When these questions are answered, people who wouldn't otherwise be added to the church (because of problems with enthusiasm or leadership) will join and contribute to a vision.

You may discover that you're meeting in a key strategic area of your city near where local government officials meet or near the biggest high school in town. You may find that the people of your church are interested in missions and want to be trained to reach out to foreign countries. The Holy Spirit might make it clear that your church is going to be strong in evangelism. In this stage, you'll begin to narrow your options and find a clear direction for the identity of your church.

In the first few months of New Life, we clearly established our church on a life-giving understanding of the Bible, worship and outreach. But our specific direction wasn't yet established. One day when I was in a hotel room, praying and fasting, I began to notice that I had been shaking my hands as I was pacing and praying. I knew that people who do this were often trying to get rid of guilt, so I started to pray about failures in my life and tried to discern what sin the Lord was trying to bring to the surface.

Then the Lord directed me to Ezekiel 3:16-21, which reads:

At the end of seven days the word of the LORD came to me: "Son of man, I have made you a watchman for the house of Israel; so hear the word I speak and give them warning from me. When I say to a wicked man, 'You will surely die,' and you do not warn him or speak out to dissuade him from his evil ways in order to save his life, that wicked man will die for his sin, and I will hold you accountable for his blood. But if you do warn the wicked man and he does not turn from his wickedness or from his evil ways, he will die for his sin; but you will have saved yourself.

Again, when a righteous man turns from his righteousness and does evil, and I put a stumbling block before him, he will die. Since you did not warn him, he will die for his sin. The righteous things he did will not be remembered, and I will hold you accountable for his blood. But if you do warn the righteous man not to sin and he does not sin, he will surely live because he took warning, and you will have saved yourself.

When I read this text, I knew that God was speaking to me about Colorado Springs. Understand that at the time we were a handful of people meeting in a basement. But after this experience, I knew that God was holding me responsible for the gospel being heard by the citizens of Colorado Springs. He said to me, "If anyone lives in this city for more than 12 months and doesn't hear a clear explanation of the gospel, and they die and miss heaven, you are responsible. If they hear and reject my message, they are responsible."

I knew that our church, no matter how successful it would become, could never clearly communicate the message of the gospel to the whole city. So that day, in my mind, the importance of churches growing and prospering all over the city took on great significance. All of a sudden I didn't consider myself responsible to encourage only those who attended little New Life Church—I knew I was responsible for the encouragement of Christians throughout the city so they would be aggressive in spreading the gospel. I could no longer just pastor the church; I needed to pastor the city.

This impacted the direction and vision of the church. Suddenly our church was broad-based and interested in the Body of Christ citywide. We invested in other churches, attended events at other

NEWARK REVIVAL

churches and wanted to grow through conversion growth and do all we could to encourage other churches to do the same.

This is why we wanted to prayerwalk the city. It wasn't a good idea I had read about—it was desperation. The direction the Lord established in our church was clear: We were ordained to make it hard to go to hell from Colorado Springs. Thus, our adventure took on a new strength.

Now, looking back on this stage, I think the Lord gave direction to the apostolic anointing He had already placed within the church. I think apostolic churches are regional churches; they think in terms of helping the broad-based Body of Christ within an entire region. The size of a church isn't always a characteristic of apostolic ministry, but regional concern and love for the Body of Christ is.

Stage Two Crisis: Autonomy

As you define your direction, your staff and church will grow. This will transform your church from a small group that can easily communicate with each other about everything to a large group of individuals (including staff and church members) who will need to check with others about some issues. Your key people will learn what roles they play, what roles you play and what they have been empowered to do. I know some pastors who let everything come across their desk to be approved, which limits their time and ability to serve the people of the church. I know others who let too much happen independently of their leadership.

When I was a youth pastor, I remember being required to change from an attitude of independence to one of interdependence as our church grew. When I first arrived, I didn't have to ask anyone if I could use the church bus. I could use it, fill it up with gas and clean it at will. One day the senior pastor told me I could no longer use the bus at will, because other people also wanted to use it. I experienced the autonomy crisis.

This same thing happens with every new employee and in every department of an organization. They ask themselves questions like, How much can I spend on items for the nursery without asking? Can I use the church kitchen on Sunday mornings without asking anyone? Do I need to ask about an announcement for the bulletin, or do I have the authority to give it to the secretary? What should I ask about, and what should I go ahead and do without asking?

The autonomy crisis happens for a number of reasons, one of which is the value of time. You and your key leaders cannot be bogged down with unnecessary meetings or with having to approve things that could be taken care of without your help. This crisis is an opportunity for you to clearly define what you can and cannot do in your own area of ministry. If you get through this period successfully, you will flow naturally into the next stage, where responsibility is delegated to the right people.

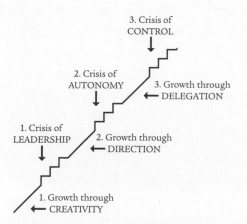

Stage Three Growth: Delegation

Churches are free to grow when the mystery of delegation is mastered by the church and its staff. This stage is exciting because it liberates people and helps them to do what they are actually called to do in order and in chain-of-command. Here, people learn what they can do without asking and what they need to ask about. They have tasks to fulfill, and they clearly understand what those tasks are and what is required to complete them.

Clearly defined delegation increases the efficiency of teamwork. It lets the individuals within the team know where they can take charge and lead and where they need to bounce things off other members. At New Life, we try to delegate as much as possible. This is where the rubber meets the road for pastors who have difficulty trusting their subordinates to do a good job without their input.

If this stage is misunderstood, it can embarrass people who do something with good intentions only to learn they weren't supposed to do it. Of course, sometimes people intentionally overstep boundaries, which moves into the crisis of stage three: control.

Stage Three Crisis: Control

Even when people overstep the boundaries on purpose, usually the best thing to do is to treat them as if you thought they did it innocently. They are trying to figure out who has authority over what, and they will make mistakes along the way. Deal with the matter privately and respond to them with a life-giving attitude. Coach them and help them figure out how to do their job appropriately.

Every church deals with control in big and small ways. We have all heard stories of the lady who has been in charge of the church kitchen for 15 years and works to maintain control over it. When someone wants to use the kitchen, she makes them sign up. She's there to unlock the door and make sure everything is done correctly. She thinks she's doing her job, but she's misunderstanding the limits of her authority and making it so that the church kitchen is hard to use.

Years ago, we had a mystery at New Life involving the toilet stalls in both the ladies' and men's rooms. The stalls were locked with no one inside. Everyone assumed that kids were playing pranks, but it kept going on for weeks.

Finally, I brought it up one day in our staff meeting. I asked if anyone had a clue how this was happening. After a few moments of silence, a little old lady named Helen, who had been with our church for years, slowly raised her hand. "Um, Pastor Ted, I'm the one who's been locking the toilets," she said.

I thought she was joking. Laughing, I said, "Now, why have you been locking the toilets, Helen?"

"Well, because my job description says I'm the one who is supposed to keep the toilets clean," she replied matter-of-factly.

Helen was doing exactly what she was supposed to be doing. She was keeping the toilets clean, but she misunderstood that the purpose of cleaning toilets was so that people would be free to use them.

Again, it's always best to handle these situations in the tree of life. Help your people understand that their purpose is to serve the people of the church and make it easy to come and worship God.

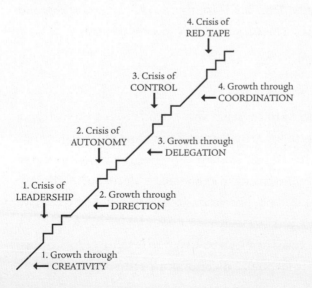

Stage Four Growth: Coordination

One of the most exciting stages of growth begins when your people start to coordinate with each other across departmental boundaries. The children's department learns to network with the youth department; the small-group leaders learn to hook up with the hospitality team and so on. Normally disparate groups begin to come together to exchange ideas, borrow from one another's resources and join forces to make a greater impact on the kingdom of God.

This is happening at New Life right now in wonderful ways. Our hospitality team has always done a top-notch job of caring for our facilities and setting them up for the many groups that meet here on a daily basis. But because we have so many different groups competing for the same space—from small groups to home-school classes, from youth meetings to worship practice—there are inevitable conflicts. Occasionally it can be awkward and require adjustments, but it's not uncommon to walk past someone's office and see people from the youth, the worship and the facilities teams all meeting together, poring over the list of rooms and discussing their various needs. They are learning to serve one another, and they realize that it's a blessing so much space is needed.

Stage Four Crisis: Red Tape

Getting people to work together always leads to red tape—forms are created and systems are put into place. How do we figure out who gets to use the van and when? Who has the right to reserve a room? Can anyone trump somone else's decision? Although our resources are limited, our needs are unlimited. So how do we make sure no one gets left out?

The red tape crisis can lead to a war. In order to explain this, I'll need to digress by briefly describing a personality profile:

At New Life Church, we use the DISC Personality Profile System for our staff and volunteers. A D person is a driver, an I person is inspirational, an S person is stable and steady, and a C person is the correct, detail person—for instance, an accountant or surgeon. As you know, everyone is a combination of these personality types, but most pastors of megachurches are dominant I's or D's, while church administrators who write the policies and practices manuals and establish the red tape procedures are primarily C's.

Thus, the importance of the team. Often the D's and I's are impatient with the C's because they want to move more quickly. To them, red tape is usually a barrier rather than something that facilitates ministry or makes people happy because the church is well organized. But if we don't design systems well at this point, our church will plateau because it is either disorganized or so cumbersome to work within that it puts people off.

At New Life, we always teach that our primary job is to make sure people are taken care of. For instance, if a small group needs a room to meet in, we want to provide that room. If the worship team is growing and needs more practice space, we need to find that space. We have written policies that guide these processes, but sometimes we have to determine whether or not the policy is getting in the way of people's needs being met. The purpose of maintaining policies is to make things run smoothly. But if someone needs something done that would violate the policy manual, then we can violate the policy manual. It's a judgment call you will have to defend later, but you can learn how to make good calls.

A few years ago, I was speaking at a conference at a large church. Not long before I was to speak, I realized I needed a white board. I asked one of the church staff members sitting near me and he looked over at the secretary and asked her where we could find one.

"That kind of thing has to be requested in triplicate three weeks in advance," she replied, not even turning around to face us.

This place is going to decline, I thought to myself. I knew it was a sign that the church was working with the wrong philosophy.

Soon after, I was speaking at another church in Toronto, Canada. Once again, I was five minutes away from speaking when I realized there was no white board for me to use. I asked the man next to me, and he immediately grabbed his radio and called to someone to bring a white board and markers to the room. There was a momentary pause, and then the man spoke into his radio again: "Well, then, unscrew it from the wall and bring it over!"

Today, the latter church continues to flourish, while the former is in sharp decline. The latter church knew how to cut the red tape to serve people; but the former is stuck in Stage Four Crisis and may never recover.

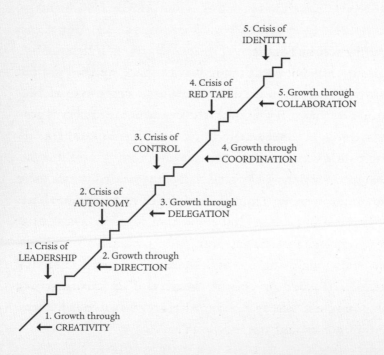

Stage Five Growth: Collaboration

Once various people and departments in your church learn to coordinate their systems, they can take the next logical step and begin to collaborate—they can use each other's resources to make the whole church stronger. Seemingly separate departments with separate visions will find ways they can plug into one another's work for mutual benefit.

At New Life, we have discovered that the youth of our church love to worship God. The worship portion of the youth meeting is always alive and exciting as teenagers and college students passionately cry out to God. As a result, a natural relationship is forming between the people on the worship team and the people in the youth department. They're linking arms and borrowing from one another's perspectives, and both of their ministries are evolving creatively because of it.

Stage Five Crisis: Identity

Once your different groups begin to work well together, you can run into a dangerous place where individuals begin to think they can leave (or just not work as hard) because the system is running so well. But every member is vitally important, and it's essential that your people know their value.

Right now in America, all the old-time sports journalists are complaining that the games have changed as professional athletes have become more and more individualistic. Basketball teams aren't really teams anymore, they complain—they are sets of five individuals who are fighting for recognition or leaving because they don't get enough "respect." The journalists are right. The games have changed as whole-team philosophies have been replaced by rampant individualism.

When this happens in a church, it can be the beginning of serious trouble if not handled appropriately.

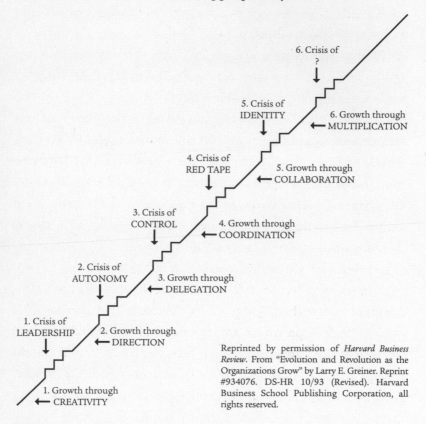

6. Crisis of
?

5. Crisis of
IDENTITY

6. Growth through
← MULTIPLICATION

4. Crisis of
RED TAPE

5. Growth through
← COLLABORATION

3. Crisis of
CONTROL

4. Growth through
← COORDINATION

2. Crisis of
AUTONOMY

3. Growth through
← DELEGATION

1. Crisis of
LEADERSHIP

2. Growth through
← DIRECTION

1. Growth through
← CREATIVITY

Stage Six Growth: Multiplication

This stage is when the church is multiplying itself. Our church is in this stage right now. We have 650 small groups, a booming youth group, a happy children's department, and tens of thousands attending our special Christmas, Easter and National Day of Prayer events. The church is growing by itself. We don't need to be under pressure every weekend because we know the church is on a healthy growth and assimilation curve.

But we also have to be aware that every new employee needs to go through the entire process of crisis and growth. I think it takes about two years. The saying around our church is, "Your first day on the job lasts two years." In addition, every department needs to go through this process to one degree or another as it grows and develops.

One of the tricks to getting through these stages is recognizing them for what they are. Especially in times of crisis we tend to point a finger at people and blame them for what looks like real trouble. We even have derogatory names for people in each of these stages: If they are in the control stage, we say they have a "Jezebel spirit." If they are caught up in red tape, we say, "You just don't get the vision. You need to hear from the Lord." But that's not the case at all. People just need training. They need to be coached. Our job is not to explain their problems to them but to assist them in living life well.

At New Life, we go over these stages every year in staff meetings. Every time we do, I can see the light turn on in people's heads. They find their own place on the chart. They also find the place of their department and the place of the church. It puts everyone on the same page, even if everyone is at different places. It helps them to understand that crisis and growth are natural and they can just stay steady through the various changes.

ETIQUETTE THAT SUSTAINS

*Do nothing out of selfish ambition or vain conceit, but in humility con-
sider others better than yourselves. Each of you should look not only to
your own interests, but also to the interests of others.*
PHILIPPIANS 2:3,4

BAD MANNERS MOCK OUR
MINISTRIES AND MARK OUR FUTURE

Several years ago, Bruce Jefferson, the youth pastor at Mountain
View Assembly, received what he believed to be a call from the
Lord to serve as a senior pastor. He began discussing his plans
with several church members who offered support, and before
long, Bruce was assured that the time had come for him to plant
a church. He hadn't spoken to his senior pastor about the matter until the day he met him in the pastor's study to announce

his departure. The senior pastor was surprised, but he accepted the decision.

Bruce started a new church with his supporters from Mountain View. Now, years later, Bruce has moved to a different town to serve in another church; and the small church he birthed struggles to survive. Mountain View has never regained the momentum it lost from the departure of Bruce and his followers. Bruce's lack of understanding about etiquette resulted in an improper response to God's call upon his life and diminished his reputation. Security in ministry is no longer an option for Bruce because he didn't practice a code of behavior that enables healthy long-term relationships.

My major fear in writing this chapter on etiquette is that I don't want to sound like the Miss Manners of the church world. God help me! But at the same time, we've all seen people who have effectively ministered the life of God to others and yet were unable to sustain their ministries because they didn't understand the social graces of the church world. The kingdom of God suffers when a believer violates decorum within the Body.

Long-term relationships cannot survive without manners. Families that enjoy harmony do so because of a code of behavior in the home. Public gatherings cannot be successful unless people have courtesy toward one another. Respecting others and knowing how to make people feel comfortable is what causes society to work smoothly. That is why we in the church world need a protocol as much as any other group.

This chapter will briefly review two sets of etiquette for Christian leaders. The first set is for the senior pastor, the second for associates. As with any other relationship, both parties must use wisdom and take responsibility for their own attitudes and actions.

Chapter Six

PROTOCOL FOR THE SENIOR PASTOR

THE KINGDOM OF

GOD SUFFERS

WHEN A BELIEVER

VIOLATES

DECORUM WITHIN

THE BODY.

___

Inter-Pastoral Friendships

When arriving in a new city, I recommend locating the ministers' gatherings and attending them regularly for at least the first year you are in town. If the pastors of the large churches attend those meetings, make a point to meet them. If they don't, call and make an appointment to meet personally with them. These pastors are the gatekeepers of the city, and their views will help you quickly orient to the community. Your presence at the meetings will help to establish a solid set of friendships that will strengthen your entire tenure in the city. After one year, go to the pastors' meetings only when you want to.

After your first year in town, you are in a position to welcome new pastors into your city. I try to get the phone numbers of pastors who will be moving to Colorado Springs so I can call to welcome them before they arrive. I offer to answer any questions they might have and assure them they will enjoy the spiritual climate and pastoral relationships within our city.

These phone calls dispel a great deal of fear and apprehension within the pastors about their new assignments and give them a friendly point of reference once they arrive.

Another courtesy that promotes interpastoral friendships is offering financial assistance to expanding churches. New Life doesn't generally send financial assistance to struggling churches, simply because it's important that free-market dynamics determine whether or not churches survive. But if a pastor's family is suffering because of a downward spiral in the church, we will sometimes send money to the pastor so his family can experience some relief.

If a neighboring church is doing any kind of construction to upgrade its facilities, we send some money to help. Or, if a church is celebrating an anniversary or a grand opening, we always send flowers and a card. Once a few churches start displaying this kind of support for one another, it becomes the culture of your city, which facilitates longevity in pastoral positions and the life of God flowing through churches—because of good manners.

Resigning

I believe senior pastors need to find their life call and stay in the same church and community as long as possible. I also believe it takes four years to meet someone, which means it also takes four years to meet a church and, in fact, it takes four years to begin substantive ministry within a church.

The standard I use to determine longevity in a church is whether or not it is growing. After the first four years of orientation, the church should begin growing steadily by at least 10 percent a year. If it does, stay. If it doesn't, try to correct the problem within the next year. If the church still won't grow, move on.

Don't blame anyone or anything, just humble yourself and learn from the experience, then try again in another city.

The exceptions to this four-year standard are obvious: a declining population in the region, a limited population base or some other influence totally outside of your control. But in most situations, this standard works.

That being said, I understand that situations arise when it is the genuine leading of God and/or a practical necessity to resign from a church. In those instances, always talk with the church leadership first, announce your departure to the congregation, and leave fully supporting the church. Nothing negative, critical, judgmental or offensive should be said in this process. And if negative attitudes have taken root in your heart, don't leave because of them. Hurt or bitterness will prevent you from growing in Christlikeness and can be the springboard for a long season of barrenness. Senior pastors should only leave when their hearts are clean.

If you are moving because of the weather, don't tell the congregation that God is calling you somewhere else; tell them you're moving because of the weather. If you were fired, don't say you received a better opportunity; tell people the church leadership felt the position was not suited for you, and that you agree. If you are tired, just say it.

Graciously, wisely and with discretion tell the truth. Don't cloak your departure in religious deception. And don't be unkind. Instead, be gracious and truthful so that every possible positive relationship can be sustained.

Hiring and Firing Staff Members

I believe that senior pastors should work for the church, and staff members should work for the senior pastor. To have an effective team, senior pastors must be able to build and trim their own staff. I hire people who have both skill and personality. I enjoy ministering with people I like; therefore, I hire my friends. I hire people toward whom I have a divine flow.

Ten people at New Life report directly to me, and they are a delight for me to work with. I encourage each of them to hire people they enjoy, so the atmosphere in the office is pleasant and we can work hard together. The friendships make the work relationships fun.

My responsibility to my friends is to assist them in fulfilling God's best plan for their lives. When their positions do not appear to be suitable, I wait six months to make sure my assessment is correct. If it is, I talk and work with them to help find the best possible alternative. In some instances we try a different position within the church; in other cases, that is not possible.

I attempt to be flexible in this process so that together we can find the role for that person which will be most productive for God's kingdom. Sometimes while we're searching, people continue in their positions at the church; other times, we let them go so they will have more time to locate a new position. Either way I maintain close communication and finance them beyond reason to assist in their transition.

Oh, one last note: no resignations or dismissals on Mondays.

Restoration of the Fallen

Structures do not restore people to godly leadership, friends do. I've never known of anyone who has fallen into sin and been successfully restored by the formal church structure. Nor have I ever seen a formal church structure wisely deal with sin, enabling ministry to continue without interruption. I do, however, know of many instances where a leader has fallen and that leader's friends have helped to heal and restore him, while the church itself didn't skip a beat.

The greatest test of character is our response to someone else's sin. If our responses are from the tree of the knowledge of good and evil, which emphasizes punishment instead of restoration, judgment instead of redemption or justice instead of mercy, then our responses might sow seeds that will ultimately destroy our own lives. But if our responses are out of the tree of life, we will not only protect our own hearts from subtle deception but will give the one who is in trouble maximum opportunity to find liberating life.

In my view, healthy relationships that go beyond the superficial are able to contain the temptation to develop sinful attitudes when dealing with someone else's sin. But simple corporate roles seldom withstand the pressure of finger-pointing and collapse into arrogance or religious high-mindedness. Friends cry with friends over failure, and get people healed; but supervisors without strong relationships seldom do.

So how do we restore the fallen? First, sin only needs to be repented of as far as it has actually gone. Forgiveness doesn't have to be asked from people who don't know that the sin ever occurred. So if a brother or sister falls, get him or her with trusted friends and have the person repent to everyone who has been violated. If the person repents, establish a simple but purposeful restoration plan, and have friends assist and monitor the recovery.

Don't punish people who repent; heal them. I don't believe that private sin requires public rebuke or removal from office if repentance is taking place. However, when no evidence of true repentance exists, then discipline is in order.

In every step of restoration, be sure to ask: What do we hope to accomplish from the action we are considering? And, Will this action produce positive results for the kingdom of God? When repentance is present, there is a time when love should cover sin. In these situations, mercy prevails over justice (see Jas. 2:13). But if repentance is not evident, then and only then should justice and judgment prevail.

Visiting Speakers

Before inviting guest speakers to our church, we make sure the following five questions have been answered:

1. *Can we pay them well?* When speakers accept our invitation, leaving their normal routines, families and all other duties to be with us, we recognize that the opportunity costs began when they started packing for the trip and that those costs won't end until they are settled back into their routines at home. So we cover all of their expenses except phone calls and personal purchases, and reward their families for their time away from home. When we invite pastors to speak in one of our Sunday services, we understand that they must be away from their churches on Sunday—a major opportunity cost that deserves to be rewarded.

2. *Can we host them well?* Different people like to be hosted differently. I like to be picked up at the airport and driven to my hotel room. Or, if I must travel a long distance from the airport, I prefer to rent a car with a good map. But I don't like staying in people's homes unless absolutely necessary. Why? Because they want to host me when I need to rest or work. I don't mind, though, meeting with as many people as possible who are associated with the reason for my visit.

3. *Can we communicate with them well?* When I travel, I want to know why I'm there, how many people I'm going to be speaking to, the appropriate dress for the event and any protocol issues that might be relevant. If communication is not clear, then I'll choose the topic I teach on, which might not fulfill my host's expectations. Therefore, clear written communication in advance is very important.

4. *Can we introduce them well?* The purpose of an introduction is to prevent speakers from having to spend the first 15 minutes of their talk connecting with the crowd. If the introduction is warm and includes meaningful information, it will communicate the speaker's right to be heard. Reading from a biography is acceptable, but reading it for the first time in front of the crowd is not.

5. *Will inviting this speaker hurt any of the nearby churches that have previously hosted this person?* Sometimes we would like to have a certain speaker but, because that person has often been with another local church, we might appear to be doing something unethical if we were to ask that person to speak at our church.

Responding to Those Who Are Leaving

One of the most difficult situations a senior pastor ever faces is the departure of a valued staff member or family from the church. I believe in dialoguing with people when they are considering a major transition. With some, the discussions should occur as between friends. With others, it should occur as a pastor talking with an associate or parishioner. Unfortunately, with some staff members, the dialogue is purely a discussion between an employer and an employee. Each of these roles has its own standards of etiquette and rules of conduct.

Most tension, however, develops when the culture of the church does not allow easy entrance and comfortable exit. My experience has been that if people have the freedom to go in good graces, they will sense a greater freedom to choose to stay. I encourage full discussion when thoughts of leaving first develop, unless of course the departing staff member or parishioner chooses not to communicate and has already made a decision to go. In those instances, the pastor should not dialogue extensively with the person, but cordially accept the decision. Don't be cold, just graciously accept it.

The only exception to this standard is when, for valid reasons, you know the decision is wrong. Then you can protest, but not as a pastor or as an employer, only as a friend. Friends can passionately discuss delicate issues such as this; however, it violates every sense of dignity, courtesy and good taste to have a pastor or employer resist the departure of a staff member or parishioner.

So how do we treat those who have gone? With decorum—kind words, gracious conversation and cordiality. Never should the senior pastor become harsh, judgmental or condemning. Instead, the senior pastor should treat those who have gone with respect and affection.

But what about rejection? I feel rejected when people just disappear or announce their decision to depart. I do, however, understand that those things will happen for good reasons and I respect that. But it is easier if I or someone else on the staff is part of the process and was a part of the conclusion. Then, no matter how we feel about the decision, at least we can understand it.

PROTOCOL FOR ASSOCIATE PASTORS

Your First Day on the Job

Every church has a secret code of conduct that everyone on staff knows about, except you, the new associate.

I'll never forget my first day of work at Bethany World Prayer Center, the megachurch of Baton Rouge, Louisiana. I arrived early as the new associate pastor: clean shoes, crisp shirt and sharp suit. I was ready to minister. But it didn't happen. Instead, brother Roy, the senior pastor, began educating me in the culture of Bethany by gently saying with a grin, "Brother Ted, go home and get some work clothes on; we'll be picking up sticks today." I understood perfectly. I was in for a series of lessons about social graces that were going to have to be caught through observation, not taught with words. It took two years.

The first day for every associate pastor lasts about two years. During this time, three relationships have to be developed. The first is your relationship with the senior pastor. Learn his personality, his moods, his likes and dislikes. Don't judge him, just serve him. Make him glad you are there.

The second significant relationship to cultivate is with other associates. They know all of the unspoken rules, so watch them closely. They understand how and when to dress; they understand when to be visible and when to disappear and how to get the job done. But they won't know what to think of you until you've been there a while, so stay steady. Have a servant's heart and yet serve with confidence. Don't be arrogant, but don't be a puppy. Just stay humble.

As these first two relationships are developing, the door will open for a significant relationship with the congregation itself. As the pastor gets to know you and the other associates begin to respect you, you will enter into effective ministry within the congregation. It will feel great; but remember, the process takes about two years.

These first two years will include lessons on personality styles, power, wisdom and patience. Building for a successful future is tied closely with your ability to patiently stay innocent as you learn. If you give the impression that you are impatient, disloyal, high-minded or just waiting for a better offer, people will only superficially connect with you. Conversely, if you make a decision to relate with people as if you're going to stay for the rest of your life, you might actually receive that option.

As you work through your first two years, develop a healthy pattern of praying and fasting, daily Bible reading and serving with confidence and humility. Don't brag or even talk much about your spiritual discipline, just do it. Make the senior pastor's job easier and understand that both of you will have different expectations as time passes. Don't let your original expectations limit you; instead, stay flexible so your strengths can find your most productive role within the church.

Multiple Roles in Relationships

If your goal is to develop a positive and healthy relationship with the pastor, you must understand the multiple roles he will have in your life: associate in ministry, friend, intercessor, defender, confidant, employer, traveling companion and basketball buddy—all at the same time. These different roles can become very confusing.

To successfully serve as an associate pastor, you will have to learn to separate these various roles. Early in the day, the senior pastor may be your friend. When he calls you that evening, he is your boss. The next morning when you see him in church, he's your spiritual leader. But on Monday when you play basketball with him, he's an old man with a bad back.

Occasionally when meeting with my staff, decorum requires that I distinguish our roles. I'll openly say that this conversation is friend to friend, or church business, or whatever. Clarifying the roles can help, but most associates usually know which role I'm in at the time.

But I Have a Call on My Life Too!

For churches to grow, many more people must be called to be associates than senior pastors. New Life Church has many pastors, but only one senior pastor. Because of my style, we function as a team; however, the buck stops with me.

Every pastor on our staff has a strong sense of purpose, and I pray that their purpose will be fulfilled at New Life. Out of love and respect for them, I do everything I can to see that their dreams are fulfilled and that the desires within their hearts are satisfied. Therefore, the vast majority of our pastors have served in various roles within our church. Communication and flexibility allow the transitions to protect everyone's dignity as the years pass and as our ministries grow.

I deeply love and appreciate every day of working with the pastoral team God has placed at New Life. Yet I understand that as they go through the various stages of life, their hearts can become restless and at times they sense the call of God to go pastor a church themselves. Even though I hate it, my responsibility as their friend and pastor is to assist them in doing what's right for them and for the kingdom of God.

Can I Work at Another Church in Town?

Yes, but certain rules apply. For example, it is improper for any leader to take a position in another church within the same city unless the senior pastor has made the arrangements to do so. When the associate has independently arranged the move to a nearby church, a major violation of protocol and a betrayal of the Kingdom occurs. It feels too much like a divorce. It betrays a sacred trust.

The sacred trust is also violated when an associate takes a senior pastor's position in a nearby church without the senior pastor's initiative. A pastor moving to a neighboring church should never confuse relationships established in another local church. Subjecting believers to awkward situations such as these is unwise and unproductive. It's poor judgment and causes believers to feel like children whose parents are divorcing. Don't do it.

I Think God Is Calling Me to Plant a Church

A worse violation of common courtesy occurs when an associate leaves to plant a church nearby. This is the ultimate violation of any sense of social grace and is an offense to God.

Associates who resign or are dismissed should not serve in a church or plant a church within a one-hour drive of their previous church. *The Haggard one-hour rule.*

But what if the senior pastor is wrong? Gene Edwards's book *The Tale of Three Kings* beautifully addresses this situation. I suggest reading it if you have a moral dilemma regarding the senior pastor.

How do you quit so you can move on? If you want to consider becoming a senior pastor or taking another position outside of the church, which would require a resignation, talk with your pastor about it. If open communication is established with the pastor and the change is the right thing to do, resigning should not be uncomfortable. It is important to leave the church in good standing. The pastor can tell you if the timing is good or if he would rather you stay for an additional few months. A request to stay more than a year would be excessive; however, I have found that when I've asked an associate to stay a few months to help the church through a particular season, the delay has generally benefited both of us.

Longevity in Ministry

Later in this book we will discuss pay schedules and structures that encourage longevity in ministry. Staying in one location for an extended period of time is not only personally beneficial to growing our ministries, but it is also beneficial for the kingdom of God.

Unless you know, without a doubt, that you are supposed to serve as a senior pastor, ask God to place you in a church with a strong calling and faithfully serve there. As the years pass, the church will develop and strengthen, and you will find that staying with the same people year after year in a growing church is deeply satisfying.

No matter where you serve, you will be successful if you remain in the tree of life, flowing in innocence and the anointing. You will then be able to maintain an environment where the gifts and fruit of the Holy Spirit provide life-giving nourishment for others and a reputation that reflects Kingdom values and Kingdom etiquette.

CHAPTER SEVEN

SMALL GROUP MINISTRY IN A FREE-MARKET SOCIETY

Let us not give up meeting together, as some are in the habit of doing, but let us encourage one another—and all the more as you see the Day approaching.

—HEBREWS 10:25

With Ted Whaley,
Director of Small Groups

By 1993, New Life Church had grown to over 4,500 regular church attendees. Our youth department was steady; the worship team was growing; we had a large group of people praying and fasting; the people of our church were growing in the Lord. Everything seemed to be clicking.

But we noticed a problem. After doing some research, we found that we were losing people every month. Our overall numbers were increasing because of new members, but too many of our folks were quietly leaving the church. Our "backdoor" loss was at 20 percent.

We were perplexed because those who were leaving didn't have a complaint. They loved the church, enjoyed the worship and appreciated the teaching. But something was wrong. They were not adequately connected. They wanted a smaller church.

So we began to pray for the Holy Spirit to give us a solution. The Baptists said we needed adult Sunday School, while the cell folks said we needed to split up the city and group people together in homes. Others recommended more hymns or fewer hymns or shorter sermons or more meaty sermons. Everywhere we looked someone had the answer. Then God began speaking to us.

One Sunday morning, I was in my office praying and preparing to teach 1 Peter. While walking back and forth, worshiping God, the Holy Spirit began to minister to me in a special way. Suddenly a paradigm shift began to take place: Instead of wanting to go downstairs and teach 1 Peter to our people, I wanted to go downstairs and teach our people how to teach 1 Peter. Instead of seeing Sunday services as a time to teach the life of Christ, I began to see Sunday services as a time to train, empower and equip people to teach others about Christ. Sunday services were a time of ministry, yes, but they could also be a time of training for ministers.

My understanding of my role as pastor was instantly transformed, as were the roles of those who attended the church. The purpose of New Life was not what God was doing in me; it was what God was doing in us. I was to be added to their ministries; they didn't have to be added to mine. I was their coach, their enabler. They were my purpose, and I was to teach them to find theirs.

Suddenly I understood Ephesians 4:11-16 in a new way. Paul wrote:

It was he who gave some to be apostles, some to be prophets, some to be evangelists, and some to be pastors and teachers, *to prepare God's people for works of service, so that the body of Christ may be built up* until we all reach unity in the faith and in the knowledge of the Son of God and become mature, attaining to the whole measure of the fullness of Christ.

Then we will no longer be infants, tossed back and forth by the waves, and blown here and there by every wind of teaching and by the cunning and craftiness of men in their deceitful scheming. Instead, speaking the truth in love, we will in all things grow up into him who is the Head, that is, Christ. From him *the whole body, joined and held together by every supporting ligament, grows and builds itself up in love, as each part does its work* (italics mine).

I realized, perhaps for the first time, that the supporting ligaments in the Body of Christ are *relationships*. If the relationships between people in the church could be strengthened and used, real ministry could take place throughout the Body. It was clear to me now that the wisdom of age and the strength of personal example were not being adequately realized at New Life Church. Too many church attendees were unnecessarily failing in their families and other areas of their lives. We had a successful church by most standards, but I knew we could do so much more if our Body could only connect. With the combined experience and insight of all our church members, there was no reason anyone in our Body should fail in any area of their lives. I knew we had to restructure the way we grouped people so they could minister more effectively to each other. We needed to get them into small groups; but I was concerned about how to do

RATHER THAN
ELIMINATE ANY OF
OUR EXISTING
PROGRAMS, WE
DECIDED TO
SLOWLY BIRTH
THE NEW BESIDE
THE OLD AND
LET THE
CONGREGATION'S
ATTENDANCE AND
INTEREST DECIDE
WHAT WOULD
LAST.

that because traditional cells had already failed two times at New Life.

At this time, a supernatural series of events began to occur. Nearly every morning for a period of several weeks, I woke up with a fresh thought on how small groups could work with the types of people who live in Colorado Springs. More new ideas would come to me in my prayer time. Each day I would go in to work and assemble a "dream team" so we could work on what the Holy Spirit was showing me. We would sit around in a room for hours with white boards, Mountain Dew and pizza, thinking through the ideas together and discussing and refining the concept of small groups for our church. Over the course of a few weeks, we rewrote the philosophy and structure of ministry at New Life Church.

Rather than eliminate any of our existing programs, we decided to slowly birth the new beside the old and let the congregation's attendance and interest decide what would last. Our young Davids (see chapter 2) loved the new idea. We were not threatening to anyone because we weren't changing anything that was already in place. We were just broadening our "cells." We didn't impose the small group system on the church; we offered it. Our small groups were so appealing that the church naturally transitioned into them. Let me emphasize: *We didn't eliminate anything that was already in place, so we didn't lose anyone from the church or from any of the old programs.* We simply let them evolve naturally and people liked the improvements.

The Free-Market Model

As I mentioned earlier, we had already gone through a couple of small-group models over the course of two or three years. First, we offered groups based on Sunday sermons. Every group had the outline of the previous Sunday's sermon with questions for discussion. Many of our people responded well, but we were only able to get a fourth of our congregation involved. So we started offering "focus groups"—small groups centered around a certain approved topic. Here again, we saw some interest, but the church didn't respond strongly. I had to sell them on both of these approaches.

Finally, we implemented a free market small-group system, where the people in our church could start a group based on just about anything and everything they could think of. I had long believed that free markets allowed people to be innovative and creative—as they were created to be—while unnecessary restrictions limited creative development and growth. Countries that have free markets allow their citizens the freedom to produce new goods and services and the market adjusts according to the needs of the people. It hit me that church small groups could work the same way. Why not let the people in the church determine the type, number and size of the church's groups? Why not let people meet with people they really wanted to meet with?

In today's society, people are naturally attracted to people with similar interests. Hardly anyone gets together with anyone else just because they're neighbors or because they work in the same building. Rather, people hang with people who like the same things they do. People gather with people in the same stage of life, with the same life calling or with similar hobbies. People who love movies hang out with people who love movies. People who have survived alcoholism or cancer enjoy meeting with other survivors. People who fish hang out with people who fish. Moms like to spend time with other moms, and businesspeople associate with other businesspeople. Long-term relationships are most quickly developed around common interests and felt needs.

As we talked about this idea, we realized that we already had free-market small groups in place—men who met to play basketball every month, women who met at the bagel shop on Fridays, high schoolers who met at lunch to pray and talk. They were already doing it. We just weren't officially recognizing it and helping them facilitate their groups.

In the fall of 1996, we kicked off our first semester of free-market small groups with 265 groups in place. The church staff was no longer developing the ideas for small groups; the ideas were created by the people in our church. Their combined creativity and expertise led to immediate growth at New Life—both in terms of sheer numbers and in terms of the health of the Body. The first year our backdoor loss shrank to 0.7 percent. Our shrinking backdoor was immediate confirmation that people were successfully connecting and finding purpose through these groups.

DIVERSITY IN IDEAS, DIVERSITY IN PEOPLE

Our small-group menu reads like a public parks and recreation booklet, and that's essentially what it is. Small-group titles range from "A Study in James," "Christian History" and "Praying for the Nations" to "Volleyball," "Mountain Biking" and "Shakespeare." Teenagers in our youth group have started groups like "Arson" and "Main Street." Our Prime Ministers (50+) have "Sunday Service Greeters," "The Brunch Bunch" and many more. These groups aren't just recreational—all interests are subjects that are used to disciple people.

Free market small groups work because they allow us to meet the various types of people of our city naturally. People don't have to come to a program on our terms; they just come to a group because they're already interested in that topic. People go to a basketball group because they love basketball, or they go to a finance group because they need to get their budget in order; once there, they can meet with Christians in a nonthreatening atmosphere.

Several years ago, James Engel of Wheaton College developed a scale describing people's spiritual condition. The scale looks like this:

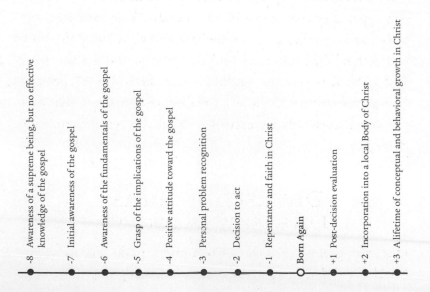

-8 Awareness of a supreme being, but no effective knowledge of the gospel

-7 Initial awareness of the gospel

-6 Awareness of the fundamentals of the gospel

-5 Grasp of the implications of the gospel

-4 Positive attitude toward the gospel

-3 Personal problem recognition

-2 Decision to act

-1 Repentance and faith in Christ

Born Again

+1 Post-decision evaluation

+2 Incorporation into a local Body of Christ

+3 A lifetime of conceptual and behavioral growth in Christ

EVERYTHING GOD

HAS DONE IN

OUR LIVES IS

UNPROVEN UNTIL

IT IS TESTED IN

THE MIDST OF

RELATIONSHIPS.

On this scale a person can move from a −8, where they barely know God exists, to a 0, where they convert to Christianity, to a +3, where they are a discipled and honorable Christian. Though not precise for everyone, the scale shows the many stages people go through in coming to Christ and highlights the fact that every individual is at a different place on the scale.

Most small-group systems minister to people who are just about ready to come to Christ or who are already Christians. That is, because church groups are for church members only, they minister to people from stage 0 to stage +3. Free market small groups, however, minister to people at all points along the scale. Our free market small groups minister effectively to people throughout the city, not just to those who are already somewhat connected to the church.

That's why the majority of the ministry at New Life Church happens in small groups. As of this writing, we have well over 650 groups that reflect the remarkable diversity of our region. Singles, couples, home schoolers, teenagers, and men and women of all kinds are accounted for within our system. (And if someone ever complains there are no groups for people like them, we simply invite them to start a group!)

The goal of this system is for everyone to move one point on the Engle scale every semester. Thus, at any given moment, 650 small groups have people moving closer to a committed relationship in Christ.

The Bottom Line

Before getting to the practical issues of our system, let me address the bottom-line philosophy of New Life Church: We respect people. We believe people have great ideas and are fully capable of leading others through life. This means that I can have a bad Sunday and it's okay. It's not up to me. Our church is about people, not Ted Haggard.

We also believe that relationships are of primary importance in any church. And by relationships, we mean dynamic, life-giving, fun, encouraging, challenging, solid long-term relationships. Everything God has done in our lives is unproven until it is tested in the midst of relationships.

The job of our church is to create solid people. We disciple people until they become disciplers. Because I am a local church pastor, I am not as interested in helping people find the latest revelation as I am in helping people establish deep roots. I get my deepest satisfaction in ministry by making people a little boring: solid, consistent and trustworthy. I want dads to be great dads and moms to be wonderful moms. Success in ministry for me happens when people pay their bills on time. My staff has done their job when people show up for work on time. This is true apostolic ministry.

THE SPECIFICS

What Type of Small Group System Should We Use?

There are a number of small-group models churches are using today. We started with Larry Stockstill's cell paradigm as presented in his book *The Cell Church*. Brother Larry explains the transition from a program-based church to a cell-based church better than anyone. When we began our transition, I sent my key staff to his church (Bethany World Prayer Center in Baker, Louisiana) to learn their system. It worked for New Life for two years and continues to work for churches across the country today.

But each church has to shape its small-group system a little differently. I recommend spending time reading some of the books that outline the various models and then shaping a system that fits with the culture of your church. Our director of small groups, Ted Whaley, trades notes with other small-group directors across the country and he's convinced that no one system has universal appeal. But what we've learned is that churches can follow models and modify them according to the size, demographics, culture and region of their church.

Variables to determine what type of cell system to use:

1. *Personality profile.* Earlier I referenced the DISC personality profile system. No one profile completely describes someone, but all of us have certain dominant personality traits. A D is a driver—a strong achiever. An I is inspirational, funny, engaging and relational. The S is steady, stable and consistent. The C is correct, detailed and specific.

   If a pastor has a high C in their personality, he will have a much more controlled and probably complex system than a high I would have. I have an ID personality, which means free market small groups work great for me. If I had a high C, I would really lean more toward the Stockstill system, the G-12 system or the traditional Cho model.

But I'm an ID who is discipling people with a high educational background who are prosperous and have never suffered. Free market cells work with this combination.

2. *Whether or not your people have suffered.* If people in your region have undergone severe trauma or suffering, they will have a whole different orientation for small groups. Dr. Cho, the pastor of the 750,000-member Yoido Full Gospel Church in South Korea, has said that the people who functioned well in his traditional cells were the ones who remembered the Japanese Occupation. Young people who had become prosperous did not respond as well to the old system. So, he developed homogenous small groups for them (which are more like free market small groups). Similarly, Bogota, Columbia, has been in civil war for several decades; the churches there use a "12,12,12" model, as in a pyramid system, which asks for lifetime commitment. For the people there, it is natural to commit to a system like that because they need security and connection. They need a Body that is tight. The middle- and upper-class people in my region would never do that. They need option and flexibility.

3. *Style/size of the church.* I don't know of any of the super-megachurches promoting cells that started as cell churches. Churches do not start out as small-

group churches; they start as program-based churches. If you are just starting, you need to develop good
programs to disciple your people. Lots of small groups
would only dilute the congregation. As the church
grows, you will be able to transition naturally to cell
groups when you need to.

4. *Economic condition/educational level of your church.* If
   your church is filled with college graduates and successful businesspeople, and you try to dictate to
   them what they are supposed to teach, they will only
   become frustrated. Make your small-group structure
   as free or as regulated as you need to for your people.
   Find ways to stimulate creative freedom and let them
   experiment; but coach when and where you need to
   coach.

It is unlikely that any one system is 100 percent replicable.
Expose yourself to a variety of systems, trust God, stay sharp, let
your system keep evolving and remain flexible. And remember
the bottom line: Assume the best of your people. The purpose is
to enable people and to release them into ministry, not to create
hurdles for them to leap over to be able to get in.

How Big Should Small Groups Be?

The term "small groups" is sometimes a misnomer. In the free
market system, there is no ceiling put on size. The number of
people in each group is left to the ability of the leader and the
interest of the people. At times this has caused chaos, but only
the type of chaos that is always a blessing. I remember a New
Lifer named Rose who decided to start a small group called
"Beginning Guitar" to teach people how to play the guitar by

using worship music. Before the first meeting even started, she received 120 phone calls from people interested in the group. She called the church in panic: "Where are people going to park?! We can't all fit in my house! This is hardly a small group!"

But Rose and her section leaders solved the problem easily. First, they identified assistant leaders to help lead the group. They relocated the group to the church for the extra space and parking. By the end of the semester, 107 people were involved in "Beginning Guitar." By that time, Rose's assistants were ready to lead their own groups and we ended up with a variety of groups that provided lessons for beginning, intermediate and advanced guitarists.

In the free market system, people vote with their feet. Multiplication and growth happen naturally and only when the size of the ministry warrants it.

When Do Small Groups Start and Stop?

We operate our small groups in semesters (fall, spring and summer, just like schools), so there are predefined start and stop dates with two-week intervals between semesters. Once again, we decide on this system because it fits with the culture of our city— the largest school districts and the colleges all follow regular semesters, meaning that many of our church members live by those semesters too.

Initially, we were concerned that a semester format might hinder long-term relationships, but it hasn't been a problem. On the contrary, 85 percent of our small groups continue to meet from one semester to the next. At semester breaks, new people are added to groups and members are given an opportunity to switch groups. So the two-week breaks between semesters benefit our small groups by giving people the comfort of knowing that their initial commitment is rather short and they can take breathers if they need to.

How Do I Structure the Leadership?

There are five levels of leadership in our small-group system: Small-Group Leader, Section Leader, Zone Leader, District Leader and District Pastor. We have separated Colorado Springs into three districts and have one pastor on staff over each district. Everyone else is a volunteer.

- At least two people and one leader form a small group.
- Five to eight small groups form a section.
- Five to eight sections form a zone.
- Five to eight zones form a district.

This is not a corporate organizational chart; it is a diagram of relationships that empower people in ministry. Sections are formed the way small groups are formed—by areas of interest (if possible). We have a section of small groups called Prime Ministers, a section of parenting small groups, and so on. So, a section leader oversees five to eight small-group leaders who usually have like interests.

Of course, all of our section and zone leaders are people who have successfully led small groups. Section leaders visit one of their small groups each week of the semester and keep in personal contact with each of their leaders regularly. Zone leaders do the same with their section leaders, and district pastors do the same with zone leaders. Strong relationship ties form. These connections are vitally important to the growth of our small groups and, in turn, to the growth of our church.

Who Is a Small-Group Leader?

Virtually anyone in our church can be a small-group leader, provided he or she meets qualifications. To be a leader, a person must commit to:

1. Serve people.
2. Meet weekly with friends.
3. Attend initial orientation and receive ongoing training.
4. Get leadership coaching with the senior pastor.
5. Tithe.

Also, all leaders must have been attending New Life for at least one year. Anyone who commits to those standards is qualified to come to the initial orientation and become a small-group leader. Staff members, trustees, elders—even me! I started a small group a couple of years ago called "Pastors' Think Tank" where local church pastors in our region met one Tuesday a month to brainstorm how to make all our churches grow. So, even the senior pastor can be a small-group leader. I love it!

How Do Leaders Get Started?

The entry point for a person who wants to be a small-group leader is a Sunday afternoon orientation meeting. Halfway into each semester we conduct a New Leader Orientation Class immediately after the last Sunday morning service. We've learned that if we provide lunch and child care, we are able to keep more people for the orientation. If we let them go home for lunch and come back, a Sunday afternoon nap easily takes precedence.

This meeting is strictly an orientation, not a training, session. During the orientation, the district pastors address the biblical basis for small groups, talk about leadership issues and answer questions and concerns. I explain the role of a small-group leader as that of a "pastor" to the people in their group. I also outline the basic tenants in our Statement of Faith, field questions about them and instruct all leaders to address issues from this position (note: they don't have to agree with our Statement of Faith; they just have to agree to teach it as if they do).

We conclude the orientation by having each potential new leader complete an application form with references, take a personality test and a spiritual gifts test, and participate in a short interview with a zone leader. All of this information is reviewed by our district pastors, who call each of the references, review the zone leader interview, review the Colorado State Background Check and make a decision to approve a new leader. If a leader is not approved because of information gained through a reference or a current sin issue, the district pastors handle it appropriately. They might suggest that the person simply participate in a group for a semester or follow some other course of action to help him or her be better prepared to be a leader. Once a leader is approved, that person is assigned to an appropriate section leader in preparation to start a group for the next semester.

How Do We Train Small-Group Leaders?

There are two common myths that exist when it comes to training small-group leaders. Myth #1 says that leaders must be fully competent and trained before leading a group. Myth #2 says that the training of leaders involves detailed skill-level training. When we first started training leaders, we required an eight-week training program on Saturdays to be completed *before* leading a group. When we saw how prohibitive that was, we whittled it down to two weeks, then to a Sunday afternoon, then to our simple orientation. Now, when someone in the church has a great idea, he or she doesn't have to jump through endless hoops en route to becoming a small-group leader. He can get started soon, while the idea is still fresh and exciting. And we can coach the person along the way.

Not everyone has a natural ability to lead, but leadership skills can be learned. Our leadership training program provides both practical skills and spiritual food. Leadership training meetings are offered the first and third Sunday evenings of each month during the semester (we started by meeting every Sunday but found it was too burdensome to the leaders' busy schedules). In these meetings, the leaders enjoy fellowship, listen to a short speaking session from a pastor or special speaker and get into what we call Section Huddles where they can voice concerns, share ideas and pray for one another.

How Do the People in the Church Plug In?

The two-week semester breaks give us the opportunity to kick off each new semester in a big way. The first week of the break between semesters is a week we call Rally Week. Several logistical purposes are served in Rally Week, such as sign-ups and letting people know details about group locations and times; but the primary function is to promote the upcoming small groups. Rally Week runs from Sunday to Sunday, with a different event attracting different segments of people each night. We may start with a Marriage and Family Rally on the first Sunday, followed by a Men's Rally Night on Monday, then the Women's Rally on Tuesday, a Youth Rally on Wednesday and so on. The worship department holds sign-ups that week; the singles group and Prime Ministers have rallies, and the children's department has an event too. Some of these events, such as sign-ups for the worship team, are geared specifically for New Lifers; but other events are for outreach (such as the youth group bringing in a band or the singles ministry hiring a professional comedy troupe).

At each event, we have tables lined up and down the main hallway of our building. Each table is hosted by small-group leaders who lead groups that might attract the segment of people attending the event. They make up their own flyers, decorate their tables, and bring food and inexpensive giveaway items to attract people before and after the Rally Week event.

At the conclusion of Rally Week, I often teach a message that emphasizes the importance of relationships within the Body. By this time, the people of the church are excited about plugging in and are ready to commit to one or more groups. Our staff and volunteer leaders spend a week following up on sign-ups, and then the semester begins.

Surprised by Results

I love the way we do small groups because it works. There is no doubt in my mind that small groups have strengthened our church. People are given many opportunities to serve, to minister and to grow, and they always respond well.

But we've also learned that small groups don't always look like we think they're going to look. In our early years, we thought every group should do everything—develop relationships, disciple people and reach out to the lost community. When we first realized it wasn't all happening in every group, we thought we should make it happen. So we tried to develop programs to make it happen. People plodded through our discipleship and outreach programs with very little passion and very little impact.

We have learned that discipleship, outreach and all forms of ministry flow naturally out of relationships. Our job is to facilitate those relationships; the ministry just happens. We can look at the diversity of our small groups and see that each group's unique flavor helps it to excel in ways that other groups won't. The hiking, scrapbooking and volleyball groups are very good at discipleship and outreach. The group that studies Henry Blackaby's Bible study *Experiencing God* is great with discipleship and prayer. We don't ask small groups to be what they're not— we just try to help them excel at what they are using to move people one point at a time, one semester at a time, toward a deeper relationship with the Lord.

CHAPTER EIGHT

LIFE-GIVING WORSHIP

How good it is to sing praises to our God, how pleasant and
fitting to praise him!

PSALM 147:1

By Ross Parsley
Worship Pastor, New Life Church

Gregg was a peculiar fellow who knew how to play the guitar and
lead worship but wasn't much interested in a steady job. He
would show up for services—having thumbed a ride in the back
of a pickup truck—with hair disheveled, his wrinkled polyester
jacket reeking of tobacco. Right before the service began, Gregg
would take a long drag on his cigarette, step inside the church—
a storefront between a bar and a liquor store—pick up his guitar

and, with hair still damp from the snow, lead the most anointed worship this side of heaven.

During these times of worship, people would be legitimately healed, delivered from demonic influences or experience God's power in their lives for the first time. There was no doubt about it—God was using Gregg at this church.

After a while, the pastor began to ask Gregg if he'd mind cleaning up a little bit. He asked him to be on time for services and to try to shower every Saturday night before church. The pastor didn't want to run off his talented musician, but he did want to encourage personal responsibility and felt his requests were easy and fair enough.

In the weeks that followed, it became clear that Gregg couldn't do it. Or he just didn't want to. Finally, Gregg came to the pastor and told him he could no longer lead worship for the church because he felt as though God had called him to lead worship for thousands. Gregg explained that his role at the little church was just holding him back.

Gregg suffered from an ailment common to worship leaders: creator complex. He wasn't the creator of the worship; he was the vessel the Creator was using. Gregg was building the worship ministry on the wrong foundation. He was relying on whatever talent he had and an anointing that God was granting instead of on solid biblical principles that moved beyond the "last great meeting" mentality.

Gregg couldn't distinguish between the calling on his life and the anointing resident within the church. He thought he was the reason that God was moving in those meetings. He didn't understand that God is not just the focus of our worship; He is also the author of it. Gregg believed that God had called him to a "greater" ministry of leading worship for thousands instead of recognizing his role within an apostolic church where God was blessing him.

Gregg was New Life Church's first worship leader. I believe he was hearing accurately from the Lord—God *was* calling him to lead worship for thousands. But he didn't realize that the place to fulfill that promise was within a local apostolic church. So I ended up receiving his promise. I got his calling! I'm the worship leader at New Life Church and I lead worship for thousands every weekend.

BUILDING ON THE RIGHT FOUNDATION

Lots of churches start worship ministries based on musical skill and then take their chances on questionable attitudes. Some choose a personality-driven model, which takes them as far as the personality clashes will allow. Some build on a foundation of musical style and let the style dictate the direction for the worship ministry, which is fine until somebody wants to change the style.

Skill, personality and music styles are all very important elements of the worship ministry. But as foundations of ministry they are shaky at best. They can't be the driving forces behind worship. Inevitably, these issues can become idols that we serve out of convenience or just plain old pride. We end up satisfied with going from service to service, hoping we can get it right and that God will move, or congratulating each other for being culturally relevant. Either way, if a music ministry is not built on biblical principles, it's the wrong foundation.

Each week our church hands out visitor's packets that contain a feedback section. Ninety percent of all those who respond mention the worship as a significant positive experience during their visit. This always amazes me—we have wonderful musicians but we are not professionals. We sing fairly well-known songs. We don't have a programming team or a worship committee. What is it that these visitors find so attractive about the worship at New Life Church?

The reason worship at New Life is so rich is because we exist on a foundation of core values and biblical principles that have protected God's anointing on the church.

Some worship ministries look like this:

Biblical principles
Ministry philosophy
Organizational structure
Musical style
Personality
Skill

This type of structure is sure to begin teetering once the storms of pride and pressure start to blow. In order to have a ministry that will stand strong in the face of emotional insecurity or church politics, we've got to make sure the foundational elements of the worship ministry are truly based on biblical principles. What we need to do is turn this pyramid upside down and place biblical foundations at the core of the worship ministry.

The worship ministry should look like this:

Skill
Personality
Musical style
Organizational structure
Ministry philosophy
Biblical principles

BIBLICAL BUILDING BLOCKS: GRATITUDE, HUMILITY AND DESPERATION

The seventh chapter of Luke paints one of the most beautiful pictures of worship and adoration found in the Scriptures. It's a story that gives us the essential lessons in worship that we need as we lead others into a deeper experience of brokenness and intimacy with God.

Simon, a Pharisee, must have been excited and a little nervous that Jesus had accepted his invitation to come to his house for dinner. That someone of Jesus' stature and fame would be visiting with him would not go unnoticed by the religious community. The real payoff, however, would come from the common people who followed the miraculous. Their recognition would ensure Simon's influence in the city.

Jesus arrived and all seemed to be going well as dinner and conversation flowed at a leisurely pace—until the arrival of an uninvited guest. A woman "who had lived a sinful life" (Luke 7:37) somehow found her way into the house and stood behind Jesus. At first no one noticed her; but then she crumpled at Jesus' feet and began crying—just a little at first, but it grew into weeping and then sobbing.

Then, without warning, she broke open a jar of perfume and began pouring it on Jesus' feet and wiping them with her hair. This was an atrocity! Simon couldn't believe Jesus was allowing this woman to touch him like that. And it almost appeared as if Jesus was enjoying it!

Just then, Jesus broke through the uneasiness with a question for Simon. "Tell me what you think, Simon," He said, and told a story about a couple of men who owed someone a lot of money.

A few in the room thought Jesus was just being polite. You know, trying to make conversation in hopes that no one would notice a crying, sobbing, wet-haired woman of ill-repute smelling up the room with the scent of nard. Others had a feeling Jesus was heading somewhere with this. Knowingly, they caught one another's eyes as Jesus went on telling the story.

Jesus finished his tale and looked directly at Simon. "Simon, do you see this woman?" He asked. The room grew tense. The disciples who were with Jesus had heard that tone before. He was about to bring the hard truth to Simon, and suddenly everyone was listening intently.

With his next words, Jesus described for Simon and everyone else in the room one of the secrets of honest, heartfelt, life-giving worship. It was right there for all of them to see, but they were embarrassed by the intimacy of it. The passion of the moment was distracting for them—it was uncomfortable. This woman had done something so beautiful for Jesus, and the only one who recognized its beauty was Jesus Himself. Simon and the others were hung up on protocol and appropriate behavior. They hadn't considered the deeper issues of decisions made in preparation for this event: the importance of the risks involved for this woman or the value of giving all that she had to worship Jesus. These matters went unnoticed by the dinner crowd, but Jesus was about to reveal the hearts of everyone in the room.

We all know the story Jesus told. Both men's debts were forgiven, and Jesus asked Simon which man would love the moneylender more—the one who had owed a little money or the one who had owed a lot. Simon answers correctly that the one who owed the most would be the most grateful. Jesus then referred to the woman weeping at his feet: "Her many sins have been forgiven—for she loved much. But he who has been forgiven little loves little" (v. 47).

If we look closely at this story, we will see that it contains the building blocks of worship: *gratitude, humility and desperation.*

GRATITUDE, HUMILITY AND DESPERATION ARE THE BUILDING BLOCKS OF WORSHIP.

Gratitude

Simon's attitude conveyed that he had no need of great forgiveness. Many churches are like Simon in that they don't have an essential foundation of gratitude toward God, and it shows in their worship. No one is overwhelmed by the Lord. Most are not in awe of Him as they sing and lift their hands. Sure, they have been taught to "enter his gates with thanksgiving and his courts with praise." But gratitude doesn't seem to penetrate their hearts. Appreciation is cursory, affection is mild, weeping is nonexistent.

Some churches struggle because they are driven by an overly intense ministry style. Everyone seems to feel the pressure of doing more, giving more and reaching for more, while rarely acknowledging the blessings God has given. The result is overblown, high-pressure worship. Other churches are permeated with a poverty mentality and seem to never get enough. They're always shorthanded for Sunday School, and the worship team struggles with commitment. The pastor and the people feel discouraged, and thus forget to be grateful for what they have. Gratitude just fades into the background. The result: weak worship.

Gratitude is the fuel for powerful, life-giving worship. At New Life, Pastor Ted places a strong emphasis on always being grateful for what you have and expressing it to God on a consistent basis. He routinely recounts the reasons on a Sunday morning—not one of us is going hungry, no one has to stand in line for food, except at a restaurant. Very few of us had nowhere to sleep the night before. None of us have to fight the police to meet together at church; no one is threatened for being a Christian. Even those who do struggle with the everyday needs of life have alternatives they can turn to for food and clothing. The evidences of God's grace are everywhere.

And, of course, God has done the unimaginable by sending His Son to die for us, freeing us from sin and restoring our relationship with the Father. If we never get anything else out of this life, that's enough to be grateful for. If we will keep our eyes fixed on who He is and what He's done for us, then our hearts will be grateful—we will know we have been forgiven and given much, and we will respond with worship.

Humility

Jesus contrasted the woman's actions with Simon's: "Do you see this woman? I came into your house. You did not give me any water for my feet, but she wet my feet with her tears and wiped them with her hair. You did not give me a kiss, but this woman, from the time I entered, has not stopped kissing my feet. You did not put oil on my head, but she has poured perfume on my feet."

(Luke 7:44-46). Jesus told Simon that he was a rude host because he failed to do the things this woman was willing to do. Simon had been thinking of his own honor and was embarrassed by the need and devotion this woman unashamedly showed.

Pride is the enemy of worship; it keeps us from taking risks. Arrogance or high-mindedness inhibits our expression of worship. Any embarrassment that we might feel in worship is pride sneaking up on us. At our church we have a saying: "Never do anything in praise and worship because of what others may think; and never refrain from doing anything because of what others may think." What God thinks is the only thing that counts.

Humility is inherent in genuine worship. The very nature of worship is the exaltation of Christ and the humbling of self. John the Baptist's words describe it perfectly: "He must increase, but I must decrease" John 3:30, *KJV*). The woman at Simon's house embodied that kind of humility. She was not afraid to humble herself before our Lord and before others, nor was she bound by the risk of embarrassment in a situation where she had much to be ashamed of.

Romans 11:36 says, "From him and through him and to him are all things." Some people think worship is from God, through them and back to Him; or from us, for Him, to them; or from us, to Him, for them. But it all begins, happens and ends with God. The desire to worship comes from Him. The ability to worship flows through Him and the glory of worship goes right back to Him. Humility reminds us that this is true—it keeps us centered on Him, not on ourselves.

Desperation

When the sinful woman knelt down at Jesus' feet, she did it out of desperation. Hers was a desperation that drove her to do something out of the ordinary, something that no one else at that dinner was willing to do. Everyone in that room was with Jesus, but only one was attending Him. Only one was worshiping.

This is how it is in some of our churches. Many are present but only a few are actually in His presence. Many are near the Lord, but some draw closer. Only a few genuinely experience Him.

Desperation forces us to go outside of the norm, to do things we would not typically do. Desperate people risk more, live on the edge and are more passionate in their pursuit. They achieve different results than those who play it safe. Yes, it can be messier and more uncomfortable than the well-traveled road; but those who choose desperation over self-sufficiency find God. And when they find Him, they find that He is pleased with their desperate hearts.

Of course, the trick is to be desperate when you don't need to be desperate. Crises always lead us back to a passionate pursuit of God because we realize in moments of vulnerabi-lity that we cannot make it on our own. We are genuinely desperate. But consider for a moment what would happen in your life, your family and your church if you found a way to be desperate for Him without having to face the crisis. What would your worship look like? How would God respond to you?

Gratitude, humility and desperation. These are three ideas that can transform your worship and your church. You can't have a worshiping church without people who are consumed with gratitude. You can't even approach the Lord without a proper perspective of who He is and how He views us—this is humility. And there will be no great display of devotion without a sense of desperation.

I have separated the three ideas here, but they emanate from the same perspective: Grateful people are humble people who know they are desperate for God.

10 Ideas That Guide Life-Giving Ministry

The following ideas are values that have been critical to building a life-giving organization and creating an atmosphere of freedom and simplicity where people can genuinely enjoy God. These are ideas that I continually communicate to everyone who joins our team. I know that if they get this philosophy down deep in their hearts, they will never have to struggle with many of the problems common to local church worship ministries.

1. The Senior Pastor Is the Worship Leader.

The senior pastor leads the church by example in worship. As the one who has been given the spiritual authority to lead the local church, the senior pastor communicates the vision and direction for everything from style to a theology of worship. Not only do people look to their senior pastor for the vision of the church, they also look at him during services to see his vision for worship. This is why I appreciate Pastor Ted so much. When people see him lifting his hands, kneeling on the floor or dancing before the Lord, my job of leading becomes easy.

As worship leaders, we are trying to lift the people to a higher place in worship, but they won't go there unless our senior pastors model worship in their lifestyles and in our churches. When people see their senior pastor abandoning himself in freedom to praise God wildly and to worship God in humility, they follow him. As the spiritual leader, the senior pastor profoundly affects the focus and participation of everyone in attendance. So, senior pastors, lead on! It will be a great blessing to your church and especially to your worship leader.

2. The Worship Ministry Must Be a Team.

Understanding team dynamics is essential for worship ministry. As the worship pastor, I love doing what I do with the team. I wouldn't want to do it by myself. The team mentality requires everyone to give up their rights as individuals for the good of the whole. We surrender ourselves to bigger goals and objectives; and because we are teammates, we each fulfill our different roles, allowing God to use us as one. Our numbers provide strength, both physically and spiritually. Of course, this means that we have no tolerance for hotshots or prima donnas. Each serves the other in humility and together we accomplish more than we ever could on our own.

Team unity is also a requirement for receiving God's blessing. Psalm 133:1,3 says, "How good and pleasant it is when brothers live together in unity! . . . For there the LORD bestows his blessing, even life forevermore." The Lord receives pleasure when we live and work together for a common purpose. When we flow together in unity, we receive a stronger anointing, greater power and, most importantly, God's blessing.

3. Leading Worship Requires Heart and Skill.

Every worship leader has to consider two important issues before he or she begins to lead: purity of heart and level of skill.

A clean heart is essential to successfully leading others into the life of God. Worship is a heart connection with God. We must be transparent and vulnerable when we come to Him. As leaders, our responsibility is to model this openness of heart as we stand before the Body of believers.

Our God-given abilities matter, too. Music, just like preaching or plumbing, has an element of skillfulness that either increases or decreases our effectiveness with others. Psalm 33:3

encourages us to be skillful, and the parable of the talents in Matthew 25 illustrates that we are responsible to cultivate the gifts and talents we have received. When we don't, we are called lazy and wicked servants.

If our music is not well done, it becomes distracting. If it is well done, people do not notice the worship leaders—they notice the Lord instead. And that is our goal. Excellent music on its own will not do anything eternal for our souls; but meeting with Jesus changes us every time. Great music under the inspiration of the Holy Spirit is an unparalleled combination to lead people into His presence.

4. Auditions Are Vital.

As the music pastor, the Lord has given me the responsibility and the spiritual authority to assist Him in inviting people to join the worship ministry in our local church. With this understanding, I ask each person to trust God and to trust me in helping them to find their place of ministry in the church. When I do not invite people to be part of the worship leadership team, I believe I am encouraging them to discover the place where their giftedness will better serve the Body and release the fullness of God's call in their lives. This is easier said than done, but it will save you and your ministry a lot of heartache in the long run.

Many people cringe at the thought of auditions. But we don't intimidate people, we help them to discern where God wants to use them in their gifts. If leading others in praise and worship is a high and holy calling, then there should be some prayerful consideration given to deciding who should be involved. When we aspire to stand before the Body and encourage worship in others, we have to balance the desire of our hearts with our talents for specific roles within the Body. God expects all of us to work within the Body and find the area where we can serve best.

5. We Must Speak the Truth in Love.

At New Life, our basis for auditions and the team mentality is Ephesians 4:15, which reads, "Speaking the truth in love, we will in all things grow up into him who is the Head, that is, Christ." Mature relationships require the truth; and often the truth sounds firm and harsh. Most of the time we get either ooey-gooey love with no truth, or brutal truth with no love. In worship ministry (as in all ministry), this is an instance where we must have it both ways—truth *and* love.

You've heard the saying, "People don't care how much you know until they know how much you care." Keep this in mind when interacting with musicians. They will respond positively, even to difficult news, if they are convinced that you care about them. If they see that you have the courage to shoot straight with them and if you demonstrate willingness to invest in them, you will earn their trust. It might be difficult, but it's worth it.

6. Music Is Just the Tool.

Music is not the purpose of the praise and worship ministry. Christmas celebrations don't drive us and Easter services are only an opportunity for more worship. All the songs and special presentations are tools for worship.

I know it's easy to get bogged down in all the work of rehearsals and preparation and planning, but we do it for a higher purpose. The rehearsals are important because the better we are rehearsed, the easier it is to use the tool of music to encourage worship. We work hard to learn the music so we can internalize the message and be free to embrace the bigger picture of what we do. We have a higher calling than just to learn music—our purpose is the worship of the Almighty.

7. We Are Only Musical Servants.

Musicians can become easily sidetracked when they concentrate too much on performance, talent or personal recognition. Our attitudes need to be the same as that of Christ Jesus, who laid down his rights to become a servant for all humankind. As musical servants to the Body of believers, we must give up our rights, our agendas and our preferences so we can concentrate on the Lord's purposes. We do not sing and play our instruments to be served and seen, but to serve and give our lives for others.

8. We Are All Worship Leaders.

The choir is not the background for the leader. The band does not just accompany the person in front. There are no "backup singers." We are all worship leaders. As leaders we have the responsibility to live worship daily. We have a responsibility to be prepared both musically and spiritually. When we stand before the congregation, we are the instruments of the Holy Spirit to inspire, motivate and encourage hearts to enter into worship. Each of us is accountable to the Lord for this ministry.

This means that we and our teams cannot be passive in leading worship. We cannot vaguely sing and play and hope that the church will join in. We have to actively engage God and connect with the congregation. We have to lead people into grateful, humble and desperate worship.

It is imperative that you explain this to your team. Knowing that they are leaders will cause them to be motivated each service instead of thinking of themselves as mere participants in the music ministry.

9. We Do Not Confuse Who We Are with What We Do.

Musicians are a strange breed—I know because I am one. We are very creative, sensitive and emotional people who at times wear our feelings on our sleeves. We tend to confuse who we are with what we do because our music is such a deep expression of our lives. But if we never learn to separate the two, we will set ourselves up for heartbreak.

We are all children of God, created in His image. We are all the righteousness of God in Christ, and we are all citizens of heaven. This is who we are. Our gifts, on the other hand, belong to God. They are simply what we do in the Body. We don't rely on our roles to give us worth. We don't use our gifts for prestige or applause.

When we can separate what we do from who we are, we can allow others to speak into our lives, to give us direction and to properly place us according to our talents and the needs within our churches. If we do

WHEN WE CAN SEPARATE WHAT WE DO FROM WHO WE ARE, WE CAN ALLOW OTHERS TO SPEAK INTO OUR LIVES, GIVE US DIRECTION AND PROPERLY PLACE US ACCORDING TO OUR TALENTS AND THE NEEDS WITHIN OUR CHURCHES.

not separate these issues, we become resistant, controlling, obstinate and proud, or we move in the other direction and become too timid or threatened to try. It is possible for us to both submit our gifts and talents to the Lord, and to allow others to speak into our lives to make us more effective in the kingdom of God. When we do this, we stay humble and openhanded, and we become a blessing to everyone.

10. Enjoying God Is Our Goal.

Church should be fun! There should be lots of smiling and laughing. People should be relaxed and feel at home. I'm convinced that many people have difficulty enjoying church simply because they take themselves too seriously. Doing church should not be our goal when we come together. Our goal should be simply to enjoy being with God and with other believers.

The characteristics of a good worship service should be the same as a good dinner with friends and family—roars of laughter, times of listening closely, discussion of important ideas. People who always approach God with a wrinkled forehead miss out on the joy and pleasure of being with the family of believers in worship.

One of our sayings at New Life is, "You know you've had a good worship service if, at the end of it, your socks are all the way down." So relax. Take a drink of living water. Enter into His rest and enjoy Him. And whatever you do, don't become so serious that you lose sight of why you're there.

CHAPTER NINE

MISSIONS: MULTIPLICATION OF LIFE

Ask the Lord of the harvest, therefore, to send out
workers into his harvest field.

MATTHEW 9:38

ONE LIFE TO GIVE

The soldiers forced the family to stand on the beach for more than an hour without telling them why they were there or what they were going to do. The family members only knew that Mom had been summoned to school earlier that day for questioning about her faith. She had been accused of telling her children about God—accusations that were true. A month earlier, during their evening meal, the mother of these seven children had told them about the Savior and His great love for them.

Everyone in the family knew the school had heard about their discussion from one of the youngest children, but no one dared say anything about it. As they stood on the beach, glancing nervously at one another and, at times, looking away in anguish, fear began to mount.

The silence was suddenly interrupted by the rumble of converging military trucks. After coming to a dusty halt on the beach, the officers exited their vehicles and approached the family, visually inspecting each family member, especially the parents. A group of young soldiers began to unload a barrel from the back of a truck and rolled it toward the water. The barrel was open on one end.

For no apparent reason, the guards lifted their rifles toward the family and forced them to stand in a row. Then the dreaded command came, ordering the mother to step forward. She handed the youngest, who had been clinging to her, to her husband. Her body quaked with fear as she began slowly walking toward the guards. Father watched in terror. The youngest, knowing that everything was very wrong, started to cry. With several rifles pointed in her direction, the officers ordered this godly woman into the barrel where her frail body was forced into a fetal position.

The mother affectionately studied her family for a few moments, then her head disappeared into the barrel. The children screamed. Daddy shouted something, but one of the guards threatened him and he stopped. Then a guard approached the oldest boy, 17-year-old Palucha, and pointed a pistol at his head, ordering him to step forward. Palucha reluctantly obeyed. The guard handed Palucha the lid to the barrel along with a hammer and nails and commanded him to seal his own mother in the barrel.

Palucha refused at first but caught his mother's eyes and listened as she softly beckoned him to obey the soldiers. She said she understood and wanted him to obey, explaining that they would see each other in another world. Palucha heaved a sob as he placed the lid on the barrel and nailed it shut.

The soldiers forced the family to watch as they rolled the barrel into the sea. The older children held the littlest ones in their arms to keep them from running after their mother. Then the guards started shooting at the barrel.

This family has never known whether their mother died from gunshot wounds or drowning. There were never any sounds from the sinking barrel. They only knew that the same fate awaited anyone in their Communist state who expressed a belief in the living God.

Afterward, the guards turned to the family and said, "There is no God. He didn't help her, and He won't help you." The trucks drove off, leaving the grieving family to stand on the beach while their dead mother sank to the bottom of the sea in her crude coffin.

FULFILLING THE PRAYERS OF THE MARTYRS

Since the fall of Communism in Europe, no one has been able to confirm this story, but when I heard it and others like it in college, my worldview changed dramatically. As a 20-year-old college student, I would walk around the campus in the evenings, asking God to use me to serve the suffering Church. I knew the martyrs had asked God to protect their families and save their countries. As I considered their bravery and sacrifice, I realized there could be no greater honor in this life than to be used by God to answer some of the prayers that were prayed in that barrel.

Just before graduation from college, I received a phone call from World Missions for Jesus, a West German missions organization. They were looking for someone to help establish a stronger North American office. When I heard that World Missions served the suffering Church in atheistic countries, I agreed to meet with them.

I accepted the position with World Missions for Jesus, and the perspective I learned there and in my subsequent position at Bethany World Prayer Center convinced me that every church should take advantage of every opportunity to impact the world for Christ. Life-giving churches do not exist for themselves but for those who don't know Christ—life Himself. God has spoken that same message to lots of people. That's why many life-giving churches are missions churches.

OTHERS, THE FOCUS OF THE CHURCH

The Bible teaches that all believers should tithe to the storehouse, which I believe is the local church. I also believe that local churches should tithe to missions. At New Life, we budget at least 10 percent for missions. But because of the way God always blesses our church, we usually find ourselves giving more than 20 percent of our total income to missions. Our church gave more than $1 million to missions last year to help answer prayers prayed in barrels.

When Jesus exhorted His disciples just before His ascension, He said, "But you will receive power when the Holy Spirit comes on you; and you will be my witnesses in Jerusalem, and in all Judea and Samaria, and to the ends of the earth" (Acts 1:8). His exhortation applies to every one of us. But the power of the Holy Spirit was not given to enable the Early Church to have better church services; it was given to provide the Church with the power to reach unbelievers. Outreach starts in our "Jerusalems," our hometowns; then our "Judeas," the state or nation surrounding our hometowns. "Samaria" is a neighboring state, in this case a despised state to the north of Judea. "To the ends of the earth" exhorts us to ensure that every people group is reached!

The reason God gives us His life is to impact our world.

New Life has a very specific strategy for staying outreach oriented. We have flags hanging in the living room—our main auditorium—from every nation on earth. We also fly the flags of Native American nations, the United Nations, the flag of the Presidential Seal, of Palestine and of all 50 states. Our church is charismatic, and because charismatics look at the ceiling of their auditoriums more than anywhere else, we hang the flags as a constant reminder to the congregation of the reason we do what we do in our living room: We are to focus on others, not on ourselves.

The World Prayer Center stands directly in front of our building. This center gathers information on Church growth from all around the world and feeds that information to intercessors.

THE REASON GOD GIVES US HIS LIFE IS TO IMPACT OUR WORLD.

We keep the intercessors of the world praying for the lost and provide them with feedback information so they know their prayers are being answered. Because the kind of praying that emanates from there is for the expansion of God's kingdom and for the continued outpouring of the Holy Spirit worldwide, the World Prayer Center is a symbol of evangelistic prayer. We want everyone who drives into our church parking lot to be reminded to pray for the lost and to focus their attention on others rather than on themselves.

OUR JERUSALEM

The first step in helping our congregation to become aware of outreach is to lead people in praying for their "Jerusalem," Colorado Springs. We often distribute a copy of the obituaries to each member of the New Life staff. On it are the words, "Today some people from Colorado Springs will be going to heaven and some will be going to hell. Our work today will affect the percentage going to heaven or hell tomorrow."

We pray through the phone book, over maps and for other churches. We pray for government leaders, schools and neighborhoods. Probably the most effective way we help our congregation to touch the lost of our city is by having them prayerwalk.

We coordinate our prayerwalking efforts with scores of other local churches to ensure that every street in the entire city is prayerwalked at least once a year.

One night my friend and I were prayerwalking through downtown Colorado Springs at about 1:30 in the morning. We were walking on a bridge high over some railroad tracks when we heard a noise on the tracks below. We leaned over the edge and saw a group of skateboarders playing on the concrete beneath the bridge. I yelled in the gruffest voice I could muster, "Hey, you boys! What are you doing down there?"

The students looked up and, after a pause, one of them sheepishly questioned, "Pastor Ted, is that you?"

I was shocked! After composing my thoughts and feeling a little embarrassed, I acknowledged to this young man who was playing with his buddies in the middle of the night that his senior pastor from the church in the suburbs was downtown playing too. My friend and I walked down to the railroad tracks to speak with them. It turned out that the boy from our church had slipped out of his bedroom window without his parents' knowledge so that he could meet his buddies. And wouldn't you know it, his senior pastor showed up! How do you explain that to mom at breakfast?

As it turned out, the boy told his parents, and his mom and dad were very grateful. Sadly, several months later his mom died and I was asked to participate at the funeral. Because of our meeting under the bridge, this young man and I were unusually connected, which made the struggle of burying his mother much easier for

PRAYERWALKING

CAUSES THE

PEOPLE OF OUR

CHURCH TO

TOUCH, SEE,

SMELL AND FEEL

OUR COMMUNITY

AT LARGE; IT

MAKES US WANT

TO SERVE OTHERS,

NOT JUST OUR

OWN LITTLE

WORLD.

both of us. We weren't strangers, nor were we limited to our church roles—all because of prayerwalking. It got me into his world; I became human to him and, I hope, a friend.

Similar stories are often told around our church. We have prayerwalking teams that target schools, certain businesses, teenage hangouts, government buildings, high places, power points and occult sites. Sometimes we prayerwalk a geographical area and other times we strategically target a site or series of sites. Either way, prayerwalking causes the people of our church to touch, see, smell and feel our community at large; it makes us want to serve others, not just our own little world.

Therefore, some of our missions money goes to our Jerusalem. We give to various community organizations that serve our community in Jesus' name. We don't have to create any organizations ourselves; instead, we partner with those that already exist but need financial assistance. Incidentally, I make a point of financing neighboring organizations, no strings attached. I don't want to serve on their boards or organize their ministries. I just want our church to help them fulfill their calling; and thus our Jerusalem is moving a little more in the right direction.

OUR JUDEA

The second charge of the Great Commission is our "Judea," which to us means our state or our nation. Several years ago the Lord spoke to me and told me to send prayer teams to every county seat in the state of Colorado. As a result of that effort, our church has enjoyed expanded relationships with churches throughout our state. Not only have many of our counties improved spiritually, but members of our congregation have connected with counties outside their normal sphere of influence and, in many cases, developed a heartfelt concern for others.

OUR SAMARIA

The next groups are outside of our region: "Samaria, and to the ends of the earth." In Jesus' day, Samaria was a region of a despised group of people from the north of Judea. When Jesus said that the power of the Holy Spirit would give His disciples power to be witnesses in Samaria, He was sending them with the gospel to people of a different culture. To do this, New Life sends people in our congregation on prayer journeys and, in a few cases, to be missionaries in the traditional sense.

In my experience, prayer journeys are the most effective way to expose the people within our congregations to the mission field. Training is unnecessary in the areas of cross-cultural communications, witnessing, conducting services or any of the other issues that would otherwise cause people to be hesitant to go. Instead, prayer journeys enhance the people's prayer lives. They begin praying together with others from their home church. Then they practice by participating in prayerwalking in their own community. Finally, they travel and pray for those living in a dark region of the world.

I enjoy prayer journeys not only because they always open the door for powerful spiritual advances, but also because they're fun. They have been packed with adventures that are too numerous to recount in detail within the pages of this short chapter. We have prayed through caves lined with bloody altars that have been used to sacrifice animals for more than 1,500 years. We have prayed in secret underground prisons once used by Communists. We have stood on the domes of Islamic mosques with both arms raised, claiming the buildings and the Islamic worshipers for Christ.

Perhaps I should take the time to tell about slipping through the dark streets in the capitals of closed Islamic nations to meet secretly with members of the underground Church in order to train them in warfare prayer. There was also the time God supernaturally opened the clouds so our helicopter could seemingly appear out of nowhere to pluck our prayer team off the top of a mountain, just in time.

Maybe it would be more interesting if I wrote about the prayer journey participant who was supernaturally protected from being hit by a bus that might have killed her, or the team members who were praying in tongues in an Islamic hospital only to discover that the patients understood them and started speaking back to them in their own language—just as in the book of Acts. The supernatural physical miracles that took place among the patients in that hospital didn't just lead to the healing of the patients, but also to the conversion of many doctors and nurses who were treating them. These high-adventure experiences are some of the reasons why prayer journeys are motivating for the people of our churches.

Prayer journeys are the penetration of God's commando forces—that's you and me and the people of our churches—into enemy territory. I've led teams to the heart of Islam, Buddhism, Hinduism and other non-Christian religions. Why? Because I don't want even one more barrel cast into the sea.

We have watched too many people bow to Mecca, burn incense, dip in rivers, slaughter animals and construct idols only to have them become worse off after their futile attempts to find God. To cancel the effects of demonic opposition and open the windows of heaven, prayer must be the number-one charge. Prayer is the way to produce a global impact.

Then we follow with strategic evangelism. In one of the nations we targeted with prayer, the Body of Christ grew 600 percent during the 12 months that followed; the growth rate the next year was 300 percent. In another nation we targeted for prayer, the underground Church was soon networked, mobilized and trained to pray through the homes, recreation sites and worship sites of its Islamic masters. We are trusting God for revival there. In our most recent "target" nation, the Body of Christ is doubling every year! Prayer journeys combined with strategic partnerships for evangelism produce tangible results every time.

The mission statement of our outreach office is "to spiritually and financially support, equip and empower missionaries and national workers who serve primarily in the 10/40 Window and among the least evangelized people groups."

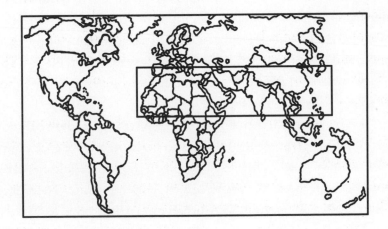

To do this, we begin with a strategy. We want to touch those areas of the world that have the greatest need and, at the same time, have fertile spiritual soil. If the soil is hard, we send prayer teams. If the soil is prepared for evangelism, we send prayer teams and develop alliances with organizations or churches that already have some work in the region and whom we can support in their efforts.

For example, in 1993, Albania was a predominantly Islamic nation ripe for the gospel. New Life Church sent our prayer team there, along with many other teams from other organizations, and enjoyed great encouragement from the Lord about the prospects for the Church among the Albanian people. Thus, upon our return home, we partnered with Every Home for Christ and the Gideons. We didn't have much financial strength at the time, so we made arrangements with both of these organizations to work through them in Albania. As a result, the kingdom of God received much greater strength through partnering than we could have achieved working independently.

Currently, I believe Nepal is ready for revival. So New Life Church is working in Nepal through five organizations that were already making headway there. We haven't had to train missionaries, buy land, build anything, hire anyone or fly anyone over there. Instead, we are working through organizations we know and trust that already have an infrastructure in place. As a result, we are seeing great results from our investment for the kingdom of God.

Strategy and partnership are the two strongest ideas behind our missions philosophy. In order to be strategic, we focus our efforts on the least evangelized people in the world. And to maximize effectiveness, we never launch projects alone. New Life Church always partners with other ministries, such as Youth With A Mission, Every Home for Christ, International Bible Society and others, or with trustworthy national brethren. With the combination of being strategic and multiplying our efforts through partnerships, we have been able to maximize our impact among some of the most difficult to reach areas of the world.

A few years ago, I was involved in a missions strategy meeting with Eric Watt, missions strategist for the Christian Broadcasting Network; Charles Blair from Calvary Temple in Denver, Colorado; Howard Foltz from AIMS; and about a half-dozen leaders of networks of churches. We were developing strategy that would incorporate literature distribution, church planting and media efforts among unreached people groups. Together we are all more effective than we ever could be alone.

When we consider training or sponsoring missionaries, we want to know:

1. Are they strategic in their thinking and planning? We recognize that every place has need, but is their destination a location of particular darkness, and are they the best resource we can send to penetrate that darkness?

2. Are they interested in training and enabling national workers to reach their own people? There is some value in direct cross-cultural ministry, but any value that is there impacts the culture more and continues multiplying for years if it includes training and empowering nationals to work within their own culture.

Once we have decided to support a missionary, we have certain guidelines that keep the relationship healthy. They are as follows:

• We do not support more than 35 percent of any missionary's total income. The only exception is if the missionary comes from our church. Then, we will support that person 100 percent for the first two years to give them time to build a support base. After two years, we limit our giving to 35 percent.

- We send all missions support on a monthly basis whether the money is sent to a missionary or to an organization that we are partnering with on a specific target.
- We give occasional one-time gifts toward specific efforts and projects.
- Our missions-support structure is simple. At the end of every year, we review the amounts and the ministries of everyone receiving missions support. We decide to either increase, decrease or eliminate their support at the end of each year.
- Then we have a balance of how much more we want to commit to missions for the next year. At that time, we review all the applications and opportunities we have received from the previous year and decide which new projects or people we will agree to help for the following calendar year.

Some of the selection criteria we use include:

a. Personal integrity;
b. Established work;
c. Good stewardship of gifts and funds;
d. Personal relationship with the senior pastor or missions director.

Once a missionary or project is on the support list, we maintain simple but informative communication with them so those on the field can spend their time doing mission work and we at home can spend our time strengthening the Church here.

INVESTING FOR FUTURE IMPACT

I believe one of the reasons families enjoy raising their children at New Life is because of our missions emphasis. Our church has a very distinct missions philosophy that purposefully directs the young people of our church.

Our children's cells (toddler through fifth grade) emphasize primary Bible education, which consists of basic Bible stories. We tell the stories of the Bible again and again, in every possible way. Many of our children's cells are held in bright rooms, using teaching tools such as puppets, actors and sometimes even popcorn. We provide maps, globes, missionaries and every possible tool to communicate the gospel message. We tell Bible stories, act them out, draw them and sing about them.

Sixth-grade through eighth-grade cells emphasize secondary application. We teach how the Bible applies to the lives of young people in this age group. In other words, we explain that because Abraham did certain things, we need to do them, too. Or because Paul said this, so must we. Our goal is that the Bible becomes personal and powerful in the daily lives of our youth. The middle-school meetings and cells all focus on learning and applying the Scriptures.

The ninth- through twelfth-grade cells teach personal purpose and local church participation with a global perspective. This group emphasizes the compelling call and purpose from God on every student's life.

In these cells, the emphasis is our personal role in the global Church. We try to take at least 100 of these high school students overseas every year. To stimulate a global conscience, they carry passports to their meetings and receive encouragement to discuss the condition of the Church in various parts of the world. They understand that God has called them to global evangelization.

We teach them strategy, city-reaching techniques, intercessory prayer, warfare prayer, networking, evangelism, and prayer and fasting.

This group is the fertile soil into which we plant seeds of loving leadership to produce a crop of Christian leaders who will love the local church and understand its role in the global Church. These students learn about holiness, calling, purpose, dying and anointing. Most churches retain about 30 percent of their high school graduates for the kingdom of God by the time they graduate from college; New Life retains more than 95 percent because of its global emphasis.

Our college meetings and cells deal with strongholds. This group tackles the major economic, theological and philosophical issues of our day and learns the Christian worldview in response. They are learning to pull down strongholds in people's minds. They are preparing to enter into adult life and either become missionaries or to support missions for the rest of their lives. After all, they are from a life-giving church, which means they are called to have a global impact.

Life-giving churches make it hard for God's children of every age to forget the bravery and sacrifice of those who have given all to lead a lost and dying world back to Jesus Christ, the giver of all life. They make it hard to forget that God gives us His life so that we can be His life-givers in Jerusalem, and in all Judea and Samaria, and to the ends of the earth.

CHAPTER TEN

CHILDREN'S MINISTRY: MORE THAN A BABY-SITTING SERVICE

Let the little children come to me, and do not hinder them,
for the kingdom of God belongs to such as these.

MARK 10:14

LIFE-GIVING CHILDREN'S MINISTRY

When I took my seat at the World Prayer Center, I soon realized this would be no ordinary memorial service. But then, Maddie Beck had been no ordinary little girl. The list of guests included Dr. James Dobson from Focus on the Family and several other leaders from our Colorado Springs community.

Maddie had suffered a rare chromosomal disorder, making her an undersized nine-year-old who loved golf balls and waffles, and who communicated not with words but by pulling people's hair. Maddie's unique personality was like that of a three-year-old, but with greater physical strength. She was a handful, to say the least. The Beck family had gone from church to church, hoping to find a place where Maddie could fit in, and where Mom and Dad could attend a service together for the first time in years.

New Life Church's children's ministry didn't have a shiny, well-designed program for handicapped children. We didn't have a special room or a highly trained "special needs" staff. What we did have was "Mr. Stan." Stan Horton is one of those thousands of volunteers who show up every weekend, in our nation's churches, because they love to teach children about Jesus.

When Mr. and Mrs. Beck first came to New Life Church, they talked with Kevin Moore, our children's pastor. He suggested that maybe they could stay with Maddie in the classroom until she got acclimated. But when he saw the tears well up in the Becks' eyes, he realized they needed some special help. Kevin heard the plea in their hearts—their need to find a place for Maddie and their desire to someday attend church together. They had spent the last nine years taking turns staying home with Maddie on Sundays.

Kevin and the Becks went to the preschool coordinators to ask their advice. The decision was to put Maddie in with the oldest preschoolers where the children were old enough to be flexible, and big enough to defend themselves should the hair-pulling start.

The next Sunday morning, Mr. and Mrs. Beck showed up a little early for preschool, and Maddie was introduced to Mr. Stan. Maddie's condition was obvious and easy to spot, and the entire classroom came to a stop to see what would happen. Instead of acting shocked or intimidated, Mr. Stan was honored to have Maddie in his classroom. He scooped her up in his arms and told Maddie that he loved her and Jesus loved her. Then he immediately began to teach the other students about how they were going to work with their new classmate. His gentle mannerisms and soft-spoken ways were the perfect antidote for Maddie's unpredictable behavior. After a few minutes, Mom and Dad were headed downstairs to church—together at last.

In the weeks to come, Maddie became central to the classroom. Young children became acquainted with ministry as they learned how to work with Maddie. They broke down the stereotypes that so often isolate special needs children from their peers. Mr. Stan never seemed to think he was doing anything unusual or out of the ordinary. To him she was just another child, another unique opportunity to serve. She was never a burden. They celebrated her presence among them. The children seemed proud of their relationship with Maddie, and she thrived in that "Maddie-friendly" atmosphere.

Months later, Maddie's condition suddenly took her home.

During her memorial service, wonderful things were spoken and the gratitude of the parents toward our church was touchingly expressed. But one of the most touching moments came when Mr. Stan stood to speak. He was clearly uncomfortable at the microphone in front of such a large gathering. His comments were very brief. When he was finished, he seemed pleased to rejoin the ranks of the anonymous. But the attitude of his heart spoke loud and clear. He still felt that he was the fortunate one, the one who had the honor of serving, the one who had the privilege of getting to know Maddie. In his heart, she was the best thing that ever happened to him.

This is a picture of life-giving children's ministry. It was no accident that Mr. Stan and Maddie hit it off so well. I believe that a number of our teachers would have also been very good for

Maddie. Children's ministry is a vital part of a life-giving church. It's not an afterthought; nor is it a necessary administration evil we have to deal with so that adults can be in the worship service. It's a key element of our weekend services, our weekday small groups and our major yearly events. Children's ministry is part of the core of everything we do because children are special to God, to parents and to us.

FOUR PRINCIPLES OF A LIFE-GIVING CHILDREN'S MINISTRY

1. Children Are Never Too Young to Start Knowing Jesus.

> From the lips of children and infants you have ordained praise because of your enemies, to silence the foe and the avenger (Ps. 8:2).

Jesus wants to be part of a child's life from the earliest possible moment. We believe that Jesus loves His little children and He can't wait for them to start knowing Him. Our children's ministry team doesn't just baby-sit or dream up time-filling activities; they work intentionally on glorifying the name of Christ in children's lives. Even in the newborn/infant rooms, our teachers pray over the children and speak biblical truths into their young lives in the name of Jesus.

The competition for a child's emotional, psychological and spiritual attention is greater than ever. Children are learning about drugs, sex and family trauma (such as divorce and domestic violence) at earlier and earlier ages. Even marketers are awakening to how impressionable and valuable is the attention of children as old as one to two years. Recently, a British television producer sparked a worldwide phenomenon by creating a television show aimed at one-year-olds, with all the characters talking in babyspeak. Everyone in the industry laughed at the idea; but before long, "Teletubbies" was one of the highest-rated shows on television.

At New Life, the classroom walls of our youngest age groups are covered with illustrations and colorful Scriptures from Bible stories. Our teachers understand that the theme of the children's ministry, no matter how young the child, is Jesus. We've built dozens of interactive prayer stations that line the halls around our children's church room, Fort Victory. Puppet skits, praise songs, clowns and object lessons all carry the same urgent understanding: Children need Jesus NOW!

WE BELIEVE THAT JESUS LOVES HIS LITTLE CHILDREN AND HE CAN'T WAIT FOR THEM TO START KNOWING HIM.

2. Children's Ministry Volunteers Are Serving God, Not the Children's Ministry.

Whoever wants to become great among you must be your servant . . . just as the

Son of Man did not come to be served, but to serve (Matt. 20:26,28).

We have all dealt with children's ministries where the volunteering process was a real chore. Even if you could find enough volunteers to fill all the slots, you couldn't guarantee that those volunteers would have a life-giving attitude. Children's ministry can be taxing. How do you keep people week after week? How do you keep them happy?

At New Life, the culture of our children's ministry has made the volunteering process much easier. People come to serve God joyfully through caring for His kids. Volunteers aren't hard to find and they aren't hard to keep. It takes work, of course, but the attitudes of our children's ministry staff and our long-term volunteers demonstrate gratitude, excitement and pleasure at the opportunity to serve God's kids. New volunteers just follow their lead and problems are few.

3. There Must Be Life-Giving Relationships Among Children's Ministry Volunteers.

Everything we've said about empowering people through small groups applies equally and especially to children's ministry. When adults are ministering to children with concentrated effort, they need relationships that are close, meaningful and satisfying.

There's no doubt about it—dealing with children can be taxing. Mistakes will be made. Serious questions will arise. When life deals the toughest blows, teachers need to know that they can find comfort, care and counsel from the people with whom they share the ministry. There is no substitute for building relationships. When misunderstandings occur, people who have strong relationships work it out. Without such relationships, they fall away. When someone becomes isolated or feels cut off, he or she can't connect with others when they really need help. One of the most important tasks of our coordinators, supervisors and pastors is to constantly build those bridges between people.

4. Children's Hearts Can Be Changed.

Every teacher has rules and expectations they teach their students right off the bat. But wise teachers know that the rules do not solve the problems; they just define the problems. Most kids, with a quick word or two from an authority, will reasonably follow the rules. But occasionally a child comes along who seems determined to break rules and challenge authority. What do you do with someone else's unruly child?

Our children's ministry staff works with the understanding that habitually disruptive students have a heart condition that can be understood and dealt with so that the children can successfully follow the rules. During one of our summer "Logotron Clubs," which is our children's ministry outreach program that takes place in public parks around town, a boy was brought to the administrative tent by one of the volunteers. He had been hitting and kicking the other kids and he refused to settle down. Warning after warning had been given, but the boy was determined to pick on his peers.

Pastor Kevin, who was busy working with the walk-in children who had just happened upon the club that day, asked the boy to join his group. The boy agreed but sat isolated from the rest of the kids, looking embarrassed and frustrated. Finally, Kevin walked over and asked him point-blank, "What's bothering you?"

The boy didn't want to say. Kevin pressed him and finally the boy told what was on his heart. He had spent the last year raising a hog. He had entered the hog in the livestock competition at the county fair and, to his surprise, the hog won sixth place. What he couldn't accept was that the hog was then sold, for a good price, to be butchered. He knew about these things. His parents had talked to him about it all along and prepared him for it. But now that it was over, his heart was broken and he figured that nobody would understand his attachment to a hog. Fortunately, Kevin handled it in such a way that caused the other kids to feel the boy's sense of loss. They asked questions and learned about hogs instead of following the camp curriculum. The boy was redeemed and caused no further problems. He had learned how to deal with his heart condition.

Of course, that boy was easier to deal with than most. But our children's ministry staff and volunteers have learned that much of the time, unruly behavior can be linked to a real problem—usually a quite simple one—that can be addressed and dealt with fairly easily. They have to deal with children's actions, yes, but they are most interested in children's hearts. They are interested in fostering life-giving relationships with kids that impact God's kingdom in a dramatic way.

BUILDING RELATIONSHIPS WITH KIDS

Our children's pastors say that one of the fundamental decisions that have shaped New Life Children's Ministry is the decision to listen to kids. Teachers build relationships with kids in their classrooms every weekend. They listen to their needs. They get to know their parents. They pray for the children's and parents' requests. Kids aren't just dropped off to be baby-sat during the service—they are left with people who care about the kids' and the parents' lives and who are interested in building lasting friendships.

Imagine what it must be like for a child going into a nursery or child care. Children love familiarity, and there is little about entering child care that is immediately familiar. The faces are strange, the toys are strange, the other kids are strange. It's difficult for parents, too, who must employ a certain amount of trust when leaving their children with church staff and volunteers.

At New Life, our child-care personnel work to gain and to build trust with the kids and their parents. We want our child-care rooms to be places where the kids look forward to going because they know the people there love them and care for them. Our staff and volunteers dive right into kids' lives; they aren't afraid to get their hands dirty and to faithfully follow through during the highs and the lows.

ASKING THE RIGHT QUESTIONS

Every children's ministry in America, including ours, struggles with the same questions from week to week:

- Can we get enough volunteers for the numbers of children we have?
- How do we lobby for a bigger budget?
- How do we train volunteers and integrate them into the classroom?
- What can we do to stop teacher burnout?
- Does the rest of the church even know that we're alive?

The culture of life-giving children's ministry at New Life has everything to do with asking the right questions. We have to address the above issues, but our ministry is fundamentally guided by a different set of questions:

- Is our standard high enough for serving in children's ministry?
- Is our ministry a blessing to the rest of the church?
- Are we appreciating our staff and volunteers?
- Does our congregation realize how much fun we're having and how much satisfaction there is in this ministry?
- Do we have enough obvious open doors to enable the people whom God calls to this ministry to easily connect with us?
- Do we articulate our needs in a number of different ways to our congregation?
- Are we accidentally sending the wrong message?
- For the benefit of all ministries in our church, how can we best stir up the gift of teaching?

THE CHILDREN'S MINISTRY IS PLENTIFUL, BUT THE VOLUNTEERS ARE FEW

Up to this point, we have only skimmed over the primary practical issue of any children's ministry: volunteers. A children's ministry is only as good as its volunteers. They are the ones who carry the load during each service. They are the ones who have to show up and serve faithfully week after week. They are the ones in the trenches with the children and parents. But virtually every children's ministry in the country has difficulty obtaining enough good volunteers to work during each service.

How do you recruit volunteers? How do you keep them happy? And how do you ensure that the job they're doing is effective for life-giving ministry?

Fundamentally, we believe that it is God's job to provide the church with the people we need to carry out ministry. We trust Him to provide people. But even if we believe that God has placed these people in our church families, then how do we encourage them to embrace His call on their lives and present themselves to us? At New Life, there are three ways the children's ministry recruits: through prayer, through intentional messages and through unintentional messages.

1. Praying to Receive God's Provision

When the classrooms are overflowing, some children's ministries make the mistake of trying to figure out where to place the blame for the lack of volunteers: the senior pastor doesn't push the ministry to the congregation; the church members are too lazy; no one really wants to do it anyway; and so on. But Jesus told us how to solve the problem of too few workers. He said, "Ask the Lord of the harvest, therefore, to send out workers into his harvest field" (Matt. 9:38). Our children's ministry considers children to be a ripe harvest field. So we need to pray regularly, in season and out, for the volunteers God has called and placed in our body of believers. We need to pray them in and trust God to do His job.

Our children's ministry makes prayer for harvesters (i.e., volunteers) a regular part of their staff and volunteer meetings. They pray for the right volunteers both at New Life and at all the other children's ministries at other churches in town. Their purpose is not just to fill the volunteer quota, but also to ask God to provide the right people at the right time with the right gifts to fill their slots. There's no doubt about it—God will call people to serve in our children's ministry. In the meantime, it's up to us to pray, trust and to serve faithfully.

2. Communicating with Your Church
Through Intentional Messages

A life-giving church shouldn't use guilt as a recruiting tool. It's true that sometimes schedule changes or the addition of new services can create immediate needs, but we don't want to be constantly sending a message of dire need aimed at guilt-ridden moms who are wanting to worship for a few minutes away from children.

The message we want to send is that children's ministry is fun. It's a satisfying, meaningful service to our risen Lord. We're storing up treasure in heaven. We have the privilege and honor to serve Jesus in this way. We enjoy the touching moments of a child's growth into salvation. We get to play with kids. In Christ, we can make a difference.

Of course, in order for us to say these things, they must be true about our children's ministry. At New Life, we have Teacher Appreciation Day every month, where we feed them goodies as they serve. The coordinators of our different areas host regular barbecues or other meetings where they bring in guest speakers to inspire or entertain. This is where the relationship-building takes place. This is where people can get the one-on-one opportunity they need to feel heard and respected and connected. At all of these gatherings we talk about the core values we share for serving children in service to our Lord.

For people who are not yet a part of the ministry, we are very intentional about announcing volunteer and resource needs.

Currently, New Life Church's children's ministry has coordinators or supervisors over the following areas:

- Nursery
- Preschool
- Elementary
- Royal Rangers
- Missionettes
- Homeschool enrichment groups
- Care for Kids (our day-care program)
- Logotron's Neighborhood Clubs (summer outreach program)
- Special Children's Events
- Resource Room
- CM Support Services

That's a ton of roles to fill! It would be easy for me or one of the children's staff members to get up on Sunday morning and talk at length about the dire need for more help. Instead, we just make the size, stature and effectiveness of our children's ministry evident. Every Sunday, church members see volunteers playing with kids in the halls, teachers transporting children from room to room in large wheelbarrows, and large colorful signs announcing upcoming children's events.

I enjoy speaking about the children's ministry from the platform. I don't have to coerce people into volunteering—I just love talking about what a great job our children's ministry is doing, and people want to help.

Of course, there are also literal announcements made through various other means, and they are always communicated in positive, friendly language. From month to month the children's min-

istry uses any or all of the following to make their presence known
and to announce their needs:

- Church newsletter
- Sunday morning written announcements
- Sunday School handouts
- Children's Ministry information booth in the church hallway
- Video ads that run between services
- Children's pastors appearing at small-group leader training
- Door posters and wall signs in the children's hallway
- Mail-outs
- Recruiting tables in the church hallway for special events
- Occasional announcements in church services

This last one is rare because our church genuinely wants to use
worship time for worship and not for announcements. If pulpit
announcements were the primary vehicle for disseminating
information, then we would lose 15 to 20 minutes per service.

COMMUNICATING WITH YOUR CHURCH THROUGH UNINTENTIONAL MESSAGES

A good sign that your children's ministry is healthy is when the
interaction with the rest of the congregation is positive and sup-
ports what you're telling people about yourselves. In other
words, when parents pick up their children, are the teachers
upbeat and positive? Do they feel supported and pleased with
their leadership? Are they being taken care of, or are they worn

out and disillusioned? Are they happy to serve, taking time to talk with parents about each child? Or is it more like, "Here's your kid—what took you so long to get here?"

Each of our coordinators has expectations of how they want their volunteers to interact with the congregation we serve. We try to staff our volunteers with an appropriate number of children so they will have time to get to know each child. We limit classroom size to a predetermined maximum number so that our teachers can be successful and feel good about the job they do. To flood them with huge numbers of children would not be life-giving; it would simply be taking advantage of a volunteer.

If children's ministry has the heart of a servant, and we find ways to genuinely appreciate, protect and encourage our volunteers and teachers, then the inadvertent messages sent throughout the church will reflect those values and people will want to serve in this ministry.

ARE WE READY TO RECEIVE GOD'S PROVISION—THE GOD-SENT VOLUNTEERS?

When people volunteer, the children's ministry must be prepared to train and integrate them as smoothly as possible. If this process is too difficult, you will lose volunteers quickly. If it's too easy, you won't be able to maintain the culture of your ministry.

A few years ago, the children's ministry at New Life was growing faster than our supply of teachers. We had supervisors and coordinators in every area ready to train new people (our training includes getting familiar with the curriculum, working alongside experienced teachers and being monitored by the coordinators). We had some new classrooms waiting for new staff. We had a system for appreciating our teachers and we were devoted to building relationships with our volunteers. But our children's ministry leaders felt that God was telling them they weren't ready for more volunteers. What was the holdup?

As they prayed during the next few months, God showed us in several different ways that our screening and interviewing process was not nearly thorough enough. The more we investigated, the more He quickened our desire to put in place a system of background checks, interviews and reference follow-ups that would maximize the safety of our children. Setting up a more responsible system almost immediately opened the doors to a steady stream of volunteers brought there by God.

The children's ministry at New Life is one of the things I am most grateful to God for. Our staff and volunteers love children and parents alike and they serve faithfully week after week. My kids have all gone through the children's ministry, and it has been a blessing to see them learn verses and worship songs and build character that will guide them as they grow up.

CHAPTER ELEVEN

YOUTH MINISTRY: HOW TO LOVE AND SERVE YOUR YOUTH PASTOR

*Be devoted to one another in brotherly love. Honor one
another above yourselves.*

ROMANS 12:10

A CRUCIAL COMPONENT OF THE LIFE-GIVING CHURCH

Recently I listened to one of the most passionate, life-giving
sermons I have heard in a long time. The speaker wasn't anyone
you would be familiar with. But after listening to him, I was
convinced he could be one of the keynote Christian speakers at
any Christian gathering. He is intelligent, resourceful and challenging. He is humble in tone, confident in purpose and colorful in manner. His topic was memorable and relevant, and he
spoke with such gracious authority that I doubt anyone in

GOOD YOUTH PAS-
TORS ARE THE
MICHAEL JORDANS
OF THE CHURCH
WORLD. IF WE DO
OUR WORK WELL
BY BUILDING A
STRONG MINISTRY
TEAM, OUR YOUTH
MINISTERS CAN
BE THE MOST
TALENTED,
INNOVATIVE,
CREATIVE YOUNG
DAVIDS WE HAVE.

the audience left untouched that day. He is my youth pastor.

It is easy to be happy with my youth pastor, or any coworker for that matter, when their performance is top-notch. When the youth group is swelling in number and kids are learning to live in Christ, I have no problem lavishing praise on the youth pastor. But as I constantly remind myself, my youth pastor isn't just any staff member. He holds one of the most important positions in the church, and it's my responsibility to ensure that he has the freedom and confidence he needs to do a fantastic job.

After years of ministry, I am convinced that the youth pastor is one of the most significant co-laborers a successful senior pastor can have. In fact, in a day when our churches are highlighting youth ministry more and more, the senior pastor-youth pastor relationship could possibly be the single most productive relationship in the church.

HIGHLIGHTING THE IMPORTANCE OF YOUTH MINISTRY

The youth pastor's job at a church isn't just a position to be filled. We make a major mistake if we ever think the youth pastor is simply another employee or a volunteer who fills a remedial role. Good youth pastors are the Michael Jordans of the church world. If we do our work well by building a strong ministry team, our youth ministers can be the most talented, innovative, creative young Davids we have. They will work the longest hours, counsel the most people and plan the events that most dramatically impact people's lives.

Unfortunately, many churches do not see it this way. Most senior pastors, board members and church members do not adequately value their youth ministers. As a result, they either recruit the wrong person for the youth ministry role or allow the wrong type of volunteer to fill the slot. This is a mistake.

Now that missiologists have quantified the remaining task of the Great Commission and life-giving churches worldwide are working together more efficiently than ever before, youth ministry has taken on new importance.

As illustrated earlier in this book, seeds of apostolic ministry anointing begin early—often while in junior high or high school. Certainly by college, the trajectory toward apostolic ministry is taking on definition in a young person's life. In order for us to ensure that the gospel is available for every people group around the world, we need an army of young men and women who can operate in apostolic strength. Where will these young people come from? The strongest of them will come from life-giving apostolic churches that are developing high-quality, genuinely spiritual, globally focused youth ministries.

But this won't happen if we keep treating youth pastors like contract labor. Some of our senior pastors replace their youth pastors more often than they say "Amen." The stereotype of youth work is often associated with dilapidated old buses, tight budgets, little or no personal income, leftover space and an inconsistent and shaky relationship with the senior pastor. It's rare to find a youth pastor who has been in his position for more than three years, and it is even more rare to find a youth group that is steadily growing year after year.

So what's the problem? Are there no good youth pastors? Is a successful youth ministry an impossible feat? Is this just the nature of youth ministry—something we just have to accept?

No, no, and no. The fact is, there are many outstanding youth pastors out there (eight of them work here). Sometimes they allow the wrong attitudes into their spirits or receive inferior modeling and find themselves giving up and leaving their youth ministry roles. Because of dissatisfaction with the structure of their churches, poor interpersonal relationships, or a need to become a senior pastor in order to make the money necessary to sustain their families, high-quality youth ministers often resign prematurely. But it doesn't have to happen.

We senior pastors just need to do our jobs better.

Ask Not What Your Youth Pastor Can Do for You . . .

When I was a youth pastor to Roy Stockstill at Bethany World Prayer Center, my dad, who lived in Indiana, suffered a heart attack. My mother called me to say Dad was in the hospital, but his condition was not serious and I shouldn't worry. Mom encouraged me to stay in Louisiana and come home for Christmas to see everyone. By then, Dad would be recovered.

After talking with Mom, I called Brother Roy and told him about the phone call and Dad's condition. He asked me to come over to his house. When I arrived, he prayed with me for my dad, told me he wanted me to go home to be with my family and gave me more than enough money for the trip. Grateful, I left on the next plane to find Dad recovering nicely in the hospital.

For a few days, my dad and I talked, prayed and laughed together. As I left his hospital room, both of us were smiling and making plans to see each other at Christmas. It never happened. Dad died two weeks later.

Because my senior pastor demonstrated his love for me in such a tangible way, I was able to spend some priceless time with my dad before he died. After that experience, I knew that Brother Roy would protect me and keep me safe. I knew he loved me, which made me want to serve him faithfully and do everything within my power to strengthen his ministry, his vision and his calling. I didn't need my own calling. My calling was to serve his calling. I was his youth pastor and I would do whatever was necessary to be trustworthy, honorable and faithful to him.

I certainly don't know everything Brother Roy was feeling and thinking during those years, but I do know he trusted me, believed in me and loved me. I know I tested his faith in me, but he persevered. He gave me the freedom to do my job well. I would mess up from time to time and even make mistakes that created problems within the church, but he would kindly coach me and cover me. Even though he was 37 years older than I was, he was a faithful friend in the truest sense. He didn't micromanage me and he wasn't overly familiar with me; he just strengthened me. Because of Brother Roy's investment in me, both as an employee and as a friend, I was free to serve.

INVESTING IN OUR YOUTH DEPARTMENTS

Part of the stereotype of youth work is that they get the worst of what's available—the smallest rooms, the cheapest vans, the least amount of money. I regularly hear of youth ministers having to work with horrible old buses that local schools have auctioned off—it's a miracle we don't end up with more young people in bus accidents. I know that most churches try to do the best they can, and certainly youth workers need to be grateful for anything the church provides; but churches need to value their youth ministries enough to provide the best resources possible.

Because of our opportunity in this generation to raise up world changers, the youth ministry has to have a priority position in the budget in terms of vehicles, equipment, staff and public exposure. People in our community know that when they become involved with our church, their young people will be more than ministered to; they will be exposed to opportunities to impact their own schools as well as other cities and other nations. It is one of our top priorities to ensure that our church members' work with their own children will be supplemented with A+ youth ministry teams.

Of course, there's a trap we need to be aware of. Sometimes, youth pastors promise a stronger and better ministry if only they could have more staff and/or more money. We senior pastors often think the same thing; but it's not true. Genuine ministry doesn't need additional staff or money. Genuine ministry happens because of a contrite heart before God. A contrite heart in the right person with the correct gift in the correct position: that's all it takes. The right person in the right place can be successful. Then, as they work well with what they have, we senior pastors should do everything within our power to ensure they have additional resources as the ministry develops.

This principle is especially important for smaller churches with tight budgets. In small churches, where meeting rooms are hard to come by and buses and sound equipment are out of the question, it is imperative to make sure the congregation is in full support of their youth pastor. If the congregation is behind the youth ministry, there will be a constant flow of vans to borrow, condos to stay in and houses available for weekly meetings.

I know of one local church in Colorado where the youth department couldn't afford to rent a campground for their annual summer camp. The church knew of the situation, cared about their youth and was working hard to find a solution. One of the church men, who was a plumber by trade, did a job for a nearby retreat center. As part of his payment, he asked the retreat center to offer the youth group a greatly discounted rate on their facilities. They consented, and the whole church celebrated as the youth got to go to summer camp.

Stories like this make me smile, because it means that church has simply inherited the senior pastor's love ministry to young people. This can happen at every church. The amount of money doesn't have to matter; what matters is a sincere desire to love and support the youth ministry and a valiant effort to invest in them at every opportunity.

A Relationship Built on Trust

In the senior pastor–youth pastor relationship, there is no single factor as important as trust. Without trust, you will never be content to give your youth pastor the freedom needed to do a good job. Without trust, you will never have peace (particularly when you are out of town or the youth group is on a trip). Without trust, your youth pastor will never be able to let his guard down around you. And, most importantly, without trust, your youth pastor will never want to be your friend.

Youth pastor John Bolin and I have a simple system regarding the amount of trust I put in him: I trust him 100 percent, and he works with integrity and never breaches that trust. It's as easy as that. Of course, implicit trust must be built over time.

But it can never be built if the senior pastor never takes the risk of believing in his youth pastor in the first place.

One of the things I enjoy doing during Sunday morning services is getting up in the pulpit and bragging on our youth department. I don't brag unless there's something to brag about. But when a ministry team in the church, including the youth ministry team, is doing a good job, I'll freely and gladly let everyone know.

"Hey, I just want to tell you about what a fantastic job the youth department is doing," I'll say, and then mention something about one of their upcoming events. Not only does this communicate to the church that the youth department is highly prized, but it also reminds John how much I believe in what he is doing.

Privately, John and I talk frankly about his job. If he's discouraged in any way, we discuss it. If he's bored with his job, we talk about it. If he's excited and feels like God is taking the youth program in a new direction, we dig through the idea together. The secret is that these conversations are not just business, they're rooted in our friendship; and neither of us is threatened by the fact that we are discussing "work" or that we're in a boss-subordinate relationship.

Part of the reason John's youth group is successful is because he's a risk-taker. He's resourceful and creative, and he's constantly trying out new ideas. Some ideas fail and some succeed, but John knows he has the freedom to try new ideas either way. He doesn't have to worry about facing me after a big (albeit rare) failure, and he doesn't have to sell me on new ideas before he tries them. I trust him to use resources wisely and do a good job, and we talk through failures and successes alike.

I have a real relationship with John, not just a corporate one. We're friends and he knows that he has the freedom to discuss his job openly. John knows he could come into my office and say, "Ted, I'm frustrated. I hate being a youth pastor, and I want to go to law school," and I wouldn't blow up. We would sit down as friends, talk about it and deal with any problems. In order for him to stay happy, he's got to know that he has the freedom to leave. But if John and I didn't trust each other and didn't work together as friends, none of this would ever be possible.

Uprooting the Second-Class Citizen Mentality

A youth pastor from Wisconsin (I'll call him Mark) told me the following story:

Mark was serving in a large church that provided a parsonage for every pastoral staff member. Because the church was growing, a housing shortage developed and the pastors of the church met to discuss the problem. At one point in the meeting, the senior pastor glanced at Mark with an idea. "Hey, I know," he said. "Why don't we just have Mark and his family move into the apartment above the youth chapel for a while?"

Mark's heart sank: The "apartment" was a tiny one-bedroom place over the youth building. In that moment, Mark lost all confidence in his relationship with his senior pastor. Because he didn't feel like the two of them were friends, he never spoke with the senior pastor about the comment. In an attempt to solve a simple problem, the senior pastor had inadvertently communicated to Mark that he and his family were not important. Within a few months, Mark was "called" to a position at another church.

John has told me that his fellow youth pastors around the country often complain of being treated like second-class citizens in their churches. The misconception is that they work less and have more free time than anyone else in the church. Their work is with students, meaning that it's "fun" and not real work.

As a result, youth ministers often receive a lower pay scale than the rest of the pastoral staff and have to do all the busy work no one else wants to do.

That's crazy! Instead of thinking of youth ministers as lowly servants, we should prize them. Senior pastors should constantly be looking for ways to reward their youth pastors and let them know how valuable they are to the church. (The only exception here is if you hired a lazy spud. If so, you're stuck! Make him do the busywork until he gets frustrated and quits.)

Why would anyone think that youth pastors have more free time than the rest of us? The vast majority of youth pastors I know are hard-working servants who are sold out to their calling. Because of the demands of working with youth, they actually have little extra time for menial tasks (though they always seem to find time when asked). Youth pastors keep late hours, get up before anyone else, volunteer more of their time and invest more of themselves into the lives of others than most ministers do. Of course, it makes sense to me that youth pastors should be hard-working: Theirs is the business of raising young men and women to become the next generation of church members and leaders.

This being the case, I advocate compensating youth pastors the same way we do the other top people on the staff, including the senior pastor. At New Life, all of us on the pastoral staff are on the same pay scale. The youth pastor, worship pastor, small group pastors, and senior pastor all start at the same rate and receive the same percentage raises.

In our weekly staff meetings, I always try to make a point of tuning in to how John is responding to the conversation. If he's being quiet and I can tell something is on his mind, I'll ask, "Okay, John, what are you thinking?" Nine times out of 10, John has something valuable on his mind, and we all benefit from what he has to say. But regardless of what he's thinking, my encouraging him to join the conversation reminds him that his opinion is valuable to me. He knows that I never hold him in low regard. In fact, he knows I think of him as being one of the most valuable people in our church.

The Importance of Friendship

If you want your youth pastor to be innovative and effective, you've got to be his friend. You can't control him, intentionally hurt his feelings or make him feel unwanted. Never micromanage him, and always make sure he knows he's a vital part of your life. Gayle and I make our pastoral staff part of our family, and we often have members of the team over for Christmas and New Year's, go on vacations with them and spend long weekends together.

A senior pastor I was talking with recently told me that his youth pastor had destroyed his church. When I asked how, he explained that the youth pastor had sexually molested a child in the community. The aftermath had left the church in shambles. I sympathized with the senior pastor but asked him if he had known his youth minister was struggling in this area. Surprised, the senior pastor replied that he had no idea.

In my opinion, that church was destroyed because of the senior pastor's lack of knowledge. We pastors need to take the initiative to befriend one another to avoid situations like this. All of us are tempted at some time in our lives, and the Bible provides ways for us to successfully deal with it so it never has to harm ministry in the community.

This is one of the reasons why I don't want any secrets among my staff. I make a point to always look into my youth pastor's eyes, not as his superior but as his friend. If I can detect any shame, depression or anxiety, I'll take him to lunch or somewhere we can talk privately. Once alone, I'll ask what's wrong. Sometimes he'll say, "Ted this is a personal issue. I don't want to talk about it." Then I'll say, "Okay, what kind of personal issue?"

The point it, I don't talk to my youth pastor like he's one of my employees or like he's the one who is responsible for making families stay in the church. He's my friend, my coworker and my partner in ministry and life. I am concerned for the things that concern him and I truly want to see God's best for him every day.

NINE WAYS TO BEFRIEND YOUR YOUTH PASTOR AND ENSURE A STRONG YOUTH PROGRAM

1. Pursue the same goals for the city and the world together.
2. Love him. Be concerned for his good.
3. Go on a missions trip or to a conference together. This provides a wonderful opportunity for the two of you to grow together through common experiences and the learning of new ideas. This also gives you a chance to read your Bibles and pray together, which will strengthen your spiritual bond.
4. Have some fun together.
5. Protect him. Make sure he takes adequate time off and has time for his family. Defend him from unreasonable demands or judgments coming from people in the congregation. Do things to ensure he knows he is valuable to you.

6. Keep him on your same pay scale and look for unique ways to bless him.

7. Maintain an air of affirmation by publicly reminding the church what a good job the youth department is doing.

8. Take the time to know your youth pastor's strengths and weaknesses. Capitalize on his strengths and work with the weaknesses.

9. Give your youth pastor plenty of opportunity to grow, to fail and to dream. When he fails, coach him a little bit. When he succeeds, acknowledge and encourage his success.

Of course, good youth ministry requires more than just incentive and friendship. It also requires good people. They have to know you, know your calling and know your vision and have the personal character necessary to mold their own lives.

Although I don't specifically look for unusual academic training, all of the guys currently serving in our youth ministry have professional degrees outside of their area of service. John Bolin graduated as a marketing major and worked for several years in secular business. Brad Parsley, our associate youth pastor, has a degree in music and directed a nationally known music group before being scooped up by New Life Church. In addition to leading one of the largest junior high ministries in the Rocky Mountain region, he is now using his degree to train a youth choir of more than 100 people. Christopher Beard, our Internship Director, has a B.A. in business and a master's degree in Christian counseling with an emphasis in child psychology. Where most young men with his education are working in treatment facilities, he is taking the brightest and best high school graduates from around the country and training them to be mentally alert, physically strong, socially magnetic and spiritually alive. All the others are equally well trained, exceptional people. In addition to practical life skills and professionalism, all of our youth pastors are continually educating themselves to become experts in adolescent development, the Bible and relying on the power of God.

Where do we find good people to minister to youth? There are three places to look: (1) in your own churches, (2) through Christian colleges and universities and (3) through Christian organizations on or near secular university campuses. If we are in need of someone for our youth ministry team and can't find them within our church, then either I or someone on my staff will schedule a time of ministry in or near college campuses. While there, our primary purpose isn't the ministry itself, but rather to look for humble, godly young men and women who love God, love people and are willing to minister through local church ministry. I never announce that I am looking for staff members, but instead make myself available to meet Christian students and trust that one of them will stand out to me. Some always do. There are always great young men and women looking for opportunities to minister in a healthy environment.

The years of allowing a love-starved, 20-something, undereducated volunteer to coordinate the youth ministry are long past. We have transitioned into a time when we need to attract and keep the sharpest and best young men and women in our community to minister to our young people. When we do that we attract strong families and we model godly living to those in need. Our churches will grow because of the strength of our ministries to young people.

CHAPTER TWELVE

ELDERS: DEMONSTRATION OF LIFE

Therefore I urge you to imitate me.

1 CORINTHIANS 4:16

With Lance Coles,
Pastor of Church Administration

Several years ago I was at a pastors' retreat where the subject of church elders was discussed. Initial responses to the topic ranged from groans to stories of reckless disasters. It was interesting to me, though, that as pastors told stories about elders within their churches who had actually created problems rather than solved problems, each of them was quick to defend the biblical role of elders.

Because these pastors were from various styles of churches, their elders served in a variety of functions. The worst stories came from churches where elders managed, rather than served, the church, or where they tried to help in delicate situations in which they could not possibly understand the relational subtleties of their decisions, which created havoc.

Some would offer a defense of the faithful elders who serve in churches all around the world. The consensus was that most elders were fine people who wanted to serve the Body, but that they were poorly placed in structures that put them in situations unsuitable for their experience.

As part of this discussion, I presented the differences between the corporate and the spiritual functions of our churches, and asked whether their elders served spiritual roles, corporate roles or both. Every one of them said both. I asked if they thought that was the problem. They thought it was. I asked for suggestions that would help. They had none.

But I did!

This chapter on the role of elders is just that: a suggestion. It's the way we structure the elders' ministry at New Life and in our sister churches, and it works well. I know that life-giving churches throughout the world structure the function of elders differently, and I'm not suggesting that our way is the way that all life-giving churches should operate. In fact, I'm convinced there is no absolutely correct way. But I do believe that some structures are more helpful to effective ministry than others.

Our elders are ministering elders, not ruling elders. They do not have any corporate power. Their role is to help the senior pastor and his staff keep the church spiritually healthy. They have well-defined functions they perform to keep our Body stable and consistent.

As all Christian leaders know, seemingly endless discussion continues about the title and role of elders. Therefore, the title has evolved to identify various offices and functions within the church, depending on the church's interpretation of Scripture and history. Despite these variations, individuals who either perform the function or are placed in the office of elder should always meet the biblical requirements for eldership:

> An elder must be blameless, the husband of but one wife, a man whose children believe and are not open to the charge of being wild and disobedient. Since an overseer is entrusted with God's work, he must be blameless—not overbearing, not quick-tempered, not given to drunkenness, not violent, not pursuing dishonest gain. Rather he must be hospitable, one who loves what is good, who is self-controlled, upright, holy and disciplined. He must hold firmly to the trustworthy message as it has been taught, so that he can encourage others by sound doctrine and refute those who oppose it (Titus 1:6-9).

Now, with 2,000 years of development since these Scriptures were written, elders fill three dominant roles for various groups.

DEFINING THE ROLE OF THE ELDER

Overseers
The first group oversees churches from outside the local Body. Some would call this group simply "the elders," others call them "apostles," "presbyters," "bishops" or "denominational overseers." I call the outside group of elders who oversee churches "overseers." Their purpose and authority are described in Article Eight of our Bylaws (see chapter 13).

Pastors

The second group of elders is comprised of the pastoral team in a local church. Because of the nature of their roles, we believe the pastoral team should serve and be recognized as the elders who manage the day-to-day operation of the local church. To avoid confusion with the third group of elders, we refer to them as pastors, but often emphasize their ability and responsibility to also serve as elders.

Elders

The third group is the subject of this chapter. They consist of men and women within our local churches who meet the qualifications of an elder and are recognized by the congregation as functioning in that capacity, but they earn their living in the community, not from the tithes of the church members. In our church, they are able to function as elders once elected by the church Body.

In our church government, even though overseers, pastors and elders all meet the biblical qualifications for elders, we have distinguished these three roles with distinct functions. As I've already mentioned, the function of the overseers is described in Article Eight of our Bylaws, and the functions of the pastors are discussed in various chapters of this book. Now let's discuss the functions of the elders.

TEN UNIQUE ROLES OF THE ELDERS

Even though elders must perform many more functions within the Body to serve it effectively, the following are identified as the 10 essentials to the effective flow of ministry to the church.

1. Teach by Living a Godly Christian Lifestyle

Elders should reflect a Christlike lifestyle that maintains the respect and confidence of the people whom they serve. We ask our elders to:

- Be responsible financially by living within their means. This includes prompt payment of all financial obligations, support of the church and faithful care of their families.
- Avoid the appearance of evil in every area of their lives, which means elders must be careful of what they watch, what they drink, what they speak, how they dress and every other attitude and action. This, too, is a stabilizing force within the church Body, as the elders model mature Christian living.
- Demonstrate personal discipline. Personal habits, proper hygiene, appropriate dress and control of eating and exercise all model healthy Christian living for others.
- Show wisdom in their ability to bring others to maturity by successfully participating in the small-group ministries of the church.

We do not want to list every detail of what a godly Christian lifestyle is, and we certainly don't want to fall into the trap of policing others, but this gives the elders an idea of what kinds of things are important in modeling godliness.

2. Provide a Prayer Shield for the Pastoral Team and the Local Church

Every Christian needs a prayer shield. But pastors and other Christian leaders, because they are at the spiritual hub of the church, need even more spiritual protection:

- Pastors have more responsibility and accountability. James 3:1 says, "Not many of you should presume to be teachers, my brothers, because you know that we who teach will be judged more strictly."
- Pastors are subjected to more temptation. Because a pastor's role requires that he be transparent and connect with people's hearts, he is subject to greater temptation than most people.
- Pastors are strategic targets for spiritual warfare. Servants of darkness single out pastors for their greatest onslaught of spiritual attack because they know they can weaken thousands of Christians by getting just one leader to fall.
- Pastors have more visibility. Because pastors are continually in the public eye, they remain under constant scrutiny and are often the subject of gossip and criticism, which places an immense burden on them and their families.

Because of the responsibility to provide a prayer shield for the pastoral team and the church, we ask all of our pastors and elders to read and apply the principles found in the book *Prayer Shield* by Dr. C. Peter Wagner—an excellent explanation of how to build protective prayer shields.

3. Defend, Protect and Support the Integrity of the Pastoral Team and the Local Church

Not only is the call to defend, protect and support the church and its leadership consistent with Titus 1:6-9, but this teaching is also consistent with James 3:5,6:

> Likewise the tongue is a small part of the body, but it
> makes great boasts. Consider what a great forest is set on
> fire by a small spark. The tongue also is a fire, a world of
> evil among the parts of the body. It corrupts the whole
> person, sets the whole course of his life on fire, and is
> itself set on fire by hell.

Elders must always be conscious of their speech and not be silent in the face of verbal attacks against the pastoral staff or the local church. This means that elders are expected to speak proactively about the pastoral staff as well as the local assembly. Negative speech is like a cancer: Once it spreads, it causes strife and a spiritually unhealthy Body.

I am not suggesting that any elder should deny or ignore the reality of sin. If for some unfortunate reason a just cause surfaces for criticism about the pastor, it should first be a matter of private prayer. If, after prayer, an elder discerns that pastoral discipline is necessary, then the procedure of how to confront the pastor is clearly outlined under number 9 of this chapter. Random discussions are not the way to correct problems; the elders are to put out such "fires" in the congregation or community and model wisdom in their own speech.

4. Pray for the Sick

The Bible is very specific about the role of prayer in the lives of the elders. James 5:14-16 says:

> Is any one of you sick? He should call the elders of the
> church to pray over him and anoint him with oil in the

THE OUTCOME OF

PRAYER IS NOT

DETERMINED BY

A SPECIFIC

FORMULA OR

APPLICATION, BUT

BY GOD. THUS,

THERE IS NO

PRESSURE ON THE

ONE PRAYING

TO PERFORM

A MIRACLE.

name of the Lord. And the prayer offered in faith will make the sick person well; the Lord will raise him up. If he has sinned, he will be forgiven. Therefore confess your sins to each other and pray for each other so that you may be healed. The prayer of a righteous man is powerful and effective.

Elders are also included in the commission of the Lord Jesus when He commands all believers in Mark 16:18 to "place their hands on sick people, and they will get well." Clearly, Christ is the healer. Thus, the one who is laying hands on the sick person in an instrument through whom God's healing power can flow.

The outcome of prayer is not determined by a specific formula or application, but by God. Thus, there is no pressure on the one praying to perform a miracle.

Hospital Visitation Protocol
We also offer our elders some simple protocol rules to follow when visiting people in the hospital:

1. Make sure the person hospitalized has requested or approves of receiving a visit.

2. If someone else has requested a visit on behalf of the sick person, have the requesting party obtain permission from the patient or a family member (if the patient is not able) before the visit. This prevents the patient from being placed in the awkward situation of either having to tell you the visit is unwelcome or of being surprised when you drop in.

3. If the patient does accept a visit that has been requested on his or her behalf, try to have the requesting party join you for the visit.

4. Do not visit a young person or someone of the opposite sex alone. The exception might be an elderly person or a person with a terminal illness who has requested a private, personal meeting for spiritual reasons.

5. Be patient and polite, not loud and self-righteous.

6. Listen.

7. Be encouraging and sensitive.

8. Pray for and with the person, encouraging his or her personal relationship with the Lord.

9. Do not attempt to give easy answers.

Procedures for Visitation

1. Before entering the room, ask God to anoint you with the power, wisdom and compassion of the Holy Spirit.

2. Ask the Lord for the gifts of healing and encouragement.

3. If the person doesn't know you, tell him or her who you are and that you are from the church.

4. Bring a gift—some candy, a Big Mac (if you know his or her diet allows it), a flower, a toy, a book or a knickknack to cheer up the room.

5. If other family members, friends or medical personnel are in the room, give them priority in visiting the patient.

6. At the close of the visit, ask if you can help either the patient or the patient's family in any way, and follow through on your offer.

7. Convey your commitment to pray for the person, and continue to offer support throughout his or her recovery.

8. Provide lots of opportunity for the patient to be exposed to the healing power of God's Word.

The following are some verses you may want to share during the visit:

He said, "If you listen carefully to the voice of the LORD your God and do what is right in his eyes, if you pay attention to his commands and keep all his decrees, I will not bring on you any of the diseases I brought on the Egyptians, for I am the LORD, who heals you" (Exod. 15:26).

Praise the LORD . . . who forgives all your sins and heals all your diseases (Ps. 103:2,3).

Surely he took up our infirmities and carried our sorrows, yet we considered him stricken by God, smitten by him, and afflicted. But he was pierced for our transgressions, he was crushed for our iniquities; the punishment that brought us peace was upon him, and by his wounds we are healed (Isa. 53:4,5).

Jesus went throughout Galilee, teaching in their synagogues, preaching the good news of the kingdom, and healing every disease and sickness among the people (Matt. 4:23).

When evening came, many who were demon-possessed were brought to him, and he drove out the spirits with a word and healed all the sick. This was to fulfill what was spoken through the prophet Isaiah: "He took up our infirmities and carried our diseases" (Matt. 8:16,17).

As a result, people brought the sick into the streets and laid them on beds and mats so that at least Peter's shadow might fall on some of them as he passed by. Crowds gathered also from the towns around Jerusalem, bringing their sick and those tormented by evil spirits, and all of them were healed (Acts 5:15,16).

You know what has happened throughout Judea, beginning in Galilee after the baptism that John preached—how God anointed Jesus of Nazareth with the Holy Spirit and power, and how he went around doing good and healing all who were under the power of the devil, because God was with him (Acts 10:37,38).

Another way to expose people to the Word of God is by giving them a book. I suggest *Healing the Sick* by T. L. Osborn, *Christ the Healer* by F. F. Bosworth or a little booklet we have available entitled *Healing Scriptures,* which is an excerpt from a Full-Life Study Bible. The booklet is replete with Scriptures regarding healing.

For those who either do not want to read or cannot read because of illness, you might want to provide a cassette tape player and tape of healing Scriptures being read. Another helpful tool is a set of Scripture posters the person can read while recovering. The posters need to be large enough to be read from across the room. Design them with brightly colored pieces of paper and laminate them. When hung on the walls, these posters will serve as comforting faith-builders to the patient.

5. Organize, Implement and Execute Licensing and Ordination Requirements and Procedures

Because ours is an independent church, our elders oversee the licensing and ordination of ministry candidates. Materials that explain licensing and ordination are available from the church office.

6. Mediating Disputes Among the Brethren

Mediating disputes is one of the greatest provisions we have in our church administration. This provision leaves the pastors in a position to minister to the people involved in a dispute without becoming embroiled in it. And it protects individual elders.

We use this system not only within our church, but also when believers from our church have major disputes with believers from other churches. In those instances, the case is heard by a group of elders selected from both churches. The senior pastors select elders who are not known to the people involved in the disputes, so neither party is quite sure which elders are from their respective churches.

According to the Scriptures, believers in Christ are to settle disputes with other believers outside of secular courts of law. The following passages give clear instructions about how we are to respond to those who disagree with us:

> Therefore, if you are offering your gift at the altar and there remember that your brother has something against you, leave your gift there in front of the altar. First go and be reconciled to your brother; then come and offer your gift.
>
> Settle matters quickly with your adversary who is taking you to court. Do it while you are still with him on the way, or he may hand you over to the judge, and the judge may hand you over to the officer, and you may be thrown into prison. I tell you the truth, you will not get out until you have paid the last penny (Matt. 5:23-26).

> You have heard that it was said, "Eye for eye, and tooth for tooth." But I tell you, Do not resist an evil person. If someone strikes you on the right cheek, turn to him the other also. And if someone wants to sue you and take your tunic, let him have your cloak as well. If someone forces you to go one mile, go with him two miles. Give to the one who asks you, and do not turn away from the one who wants to borrow from you (Matt. 5:38-42).

> If your brother sins against you, go and show him his fault, just between the two of you. If he listens to you, you have won your brother over. But if he will not listen, take one or two others along, so that every matter may

be established by the testimony of two or three witnesses. If he refuses to listen to them, tell it to the church; and if he refuses to listen even to the church, treat him as you would a pagan or a tax collector (Matt. 18:15-17).

If any of you has a dispute with another, dare he take it before the ungodly for judgment instead of before the saints? Do you not know that the saints will judge the world? And if you are to judge the world, are you not competent to judge trivial cases? Do you not know that we will judge angels? How much more the things of this life! Therefore, if you have disputes about such matters, appoint as judges even men of little account in the church! I say this to shame you. Is it possible that there is nobody among you wise enough to judge a dispute between believers? But, instead, one brother goes to law against another—and this in front of unbelievers! The very fact that you have lawsuits among you means you have been completely defeated already. Why not rather be wronged? Why not rather be cheated? Instead, you yourselves cheat and do wrong, and you do this to your brothers (1 Cor. 6:1-8).

Prior to the mediation, all parties involved must be willing to voluntarily accept the decision of the elders as binding. The elders may invite the participation of other church members who are experts in the area of disagreement. And, when a dispute is being heard by the elders, those having the dispute must agree to allow the elders to confidentially speak with members of the pastoral staff who may have some insight on the matter.

If a dispute involves money, the number of elders required will be based on the following criteria:

Amount of Dispute

- $1 to $10,000: Three elders are to hear and decide this dispute or any disputes that do not involve monetary damages. Each party will select one elder; and the coordinating elder will select one elder. Two of the three elders must agree for a settlement.
- $10,001 to $100,000: Five elders are to hear and decide disputes of this size. Each party may select one elder; the coordinating elder is to select three. Three of the five elders must agree for a settlement.
- $100,001 or more: Seven elders are to hear a dispute of this size. Each party may select two elders; the coordinating elder will select three. Disputes of this magnitude require five of the seven to settle.

The individuals who are experiencing the dispute may ask people to send letters relating any pertinent information to the elders who are hearing the case. No limit is imposed on the number of letters that may be solicited or reviewed by the elders.

Each person involved in the dispute may bring two people to testify and answer questions during the mediation. One of the elders should open the meeting with prayer. Each side may take no more than one hour to present their case. Then the elders may question those present for as long as they feel is appropriate or necessary.

When the elders are satisfied with the information they have received, they should go to a private place to make a decision. They are to collectively communicate their decision to the parties involved at the same time and in the same room. The opinions of individual elders are NOT to be expressed. Instead, all elders are only to express the final decision of the board.

After the decision has been communicated, the meeting should be closed in prayer and the elders should remain for ministry if necessary.

7. Counsel

Elders are to make themselves available as often as is reasonable to assist people within the church with biblical counsel or wisdom from their own experiences.

8. Confirm or Reject Pastoral Appointments to the Board of Trustees and the Board of Overseers

To maintain the highest level of accountability, we must set up and maintain procedures that force us to check and balance one another. One of the ways we do this is by having our elders confirm or reject the people whom the senior pastor appoints as new members of both the board of trustees and the board of overseers.

The decision to either confirm or reject an appointment to these boards is done in accordance with Article Six, Section 4, Paragraph 1 and Article Eight, Paragraph 3 of our church bylaws.

9. Contact the Board of Overseers to Initiate Investigation and Potential Discipline of the Senior Pastor

Once again, accountability should always be a top priority, especially in the lives of those who are in positions of great responsibility and leadership. There should never be so much oversight that a leader's creativity and ability to lead with efficiency are hindered; and there should never be so little oversight that a leader is made unnecessarily vulnerable to the snares of the enemy.

In our system, the senior pastor may only be disciplined or removed for one of the following offenses:

- Teaching that violates the creed of the church
- Misappropriation of funds
- Sexual misconduct

If an elder is alerted to allegations against the senior pastor regarding any of these three offenses, the elder should meet with the pastor according to the instructions in Matthew 18. If that meeting does not satisfy, the elder and senior pastor may contact any member of the board of overseers to express their concerns. The overseers may then investigate the situation in compliance with Article Eight, Paragraph 3 of the church bylaws.

10. Represent the Church to Other Churches

Most churches need representation from time to time at special events and with sister churches. In these situations, an elder may be the appropriate representative.

CHAPTER THIRTEEN

BYLAWS OF
NEW LIFE CHURCH
A NONPROFIT CORPORATION

ARTICLE ONE

Offices[1]

The principal office of New Life Church, hereinafter referred to as the Corporation, shall be located at the address set forth in the Articles of InCorporation. The Corporation may have such other offices, either within or without the State of InCorporation, as the Board of Trustees may determine.

1. If you are leasing, it is important that the principal office of the Corporation be an address that is consistent. Most states allow a residential address to be used if the meeting location is transitional. However, if you have a permanent church location, that is the address to use.

ARTICLE TWO

Membership[2]

Members shall be all people who contribute financially to the Corporation (Church). Membership is granted and recognized with voting powers once a person has been in the church long enough to receive an annual contributions statement. A contributions statement is the certificate of membership. Should one year pass without a record of contribution, membership is automatically terminated. Members' voting rights are described in Article 9, Para. 5, relating to nominations for the Board of Elders and Article 5, relating to the selection of a new Senior Pastor. Members shall have no other voting rights.

2. This bylaw is the balance between those who strongly emphasize church membership and those who have no formal membership at all.

   I believe people need to know what determines their membership in their local church, and I think the Pastor needs to know who is a member and who is not. But membership should be structured so the leadership team is 100 percent consumed with drawing people into a relationship with the Lord, not the church. Once people establish a relationship with the Lord, their natural responses signal that they have become members of the church.

   I don't think it's wise to have too many hoops to jump through or barriers to hurdle to become a member. Actually, I've observed that when people start referring to the church in the first person, "my church" or "our church" it means that their hearts have been added to the church Body. Once again, strive for balance. People need to be strongly committed to the local church without a hyper sense of obligation. That is what this article allows.

Statement of Faith[3]

Holy Bible: The Holy Bible, and only the Bible, is the authoritative Word of God. It alone is the final authority in determining all doctrinal truths. In its original writing, it is inspired, infallible and inerrant (see 2 Tim. 3:16; 2 Peter 1:20,21; Prov. 30:5; Rom. 16:25,26).

Trinity: There is one God, eternally existent in three persons: Father, Son and Holy Spirit. These three are coequal and coeternal (see 1 John 5:7; Gen. 1:26; Matt. 3:16,17; 28:19; Luke 1:35; Isa. 9:6; Heb. 3:7-11).

Jesus Christ: Jesus Christ is God the Son, the second person of the Trinity. On earth, Jesus was 100 percent God and 100 percent man. He is the only man ever to have lived a sinless life. He was born of a virgin, lived a sinless life, performed miracles, died on the cross for mankind and thus, atoned for our sins through the shedding of His blood. He rose from the dead on the third day according to the Scriptures, ascended to the right hand of the Father, and will return again in power and glory. (See John 1:1,14; 20:28; 1 Tim. 3:16; Isa. 9:6; Phil. 2:5,6; 1 Tim. 2:5.)

Virgin Birth: Jesus Christ was conceived by God the Father, through the Holy Spirit (the third person of the Trinity) in the virgin Mary's womb; therefore, He is the Son of God (see Matt. 1:18,25; Luke 1:35; Isa. 7:14; Matt. 1:18,23-25; Luke 1:27-35).

Redemption: Man was created good and upright, but by voluntary transgression he fell; his only hope of redemption is in Jesus Christ, the Son of God (see Gen. 1:26-31; 3:1-7; Rom. 5:12-21).

Regeneration: For anyone to know God, regeneration by the Holy Spirit is absolutely essential (see John 6:44,65).

Salvation: We are saved by grace through faith in Jesus Christ; His death, burial and resurrection. Salvation is a gift from God, not a result of our good works or of any human efforts (see Eph. 2:8,9; Gal. 2:16; 3:8; Titus 3:5; Rom. 10:9,10; Acts 16:31; Heb. 9:22).

Repentance: Repentance is the commitment to turn away from sin in every area of our lives and to follow Christ, which allows us to receive His redemption and to be regenerated by the

Holy Spirit. Thus, through repentance we receive forgiveness of sins and appropriate salvation (see Acts 2:21, 3:19; 1 John 1:9).

Sanctification: Sanctification is the ongoing process of yielding to God's Word and His Spirit in order to complete the development of Christ's character in us. It is through the present ministry of the Holy Spirit and the Word of God that the Christian is enabled to live a godly life (see 1 Thess. 4:3; 5:23; 2 Cor. 3:18; 6:14-18; 2 Thess. 2:1-3, Rom. 8:29; 12:1,2, Heb. 2:11).

Jesus' Blood: The blood that Jesus Christ shed on the cross of Calvary was sinless and is 100 percent sufficient to cleanse mankind of all sin. Jesus allowed Himself to be punished for both our sinfulness and our sins, enabling all those who believe to be free from the penalty of sin, which is death (see 1 John 1:7; Rev. 1:5; 5:9; Col. 1:20; Rom. 3:10-12,23; 5:9; John 1:29).

Jesus Christ Indwells All Believers: Christians are people who have invited the Lord Jesus Christ to come and live inside them by His Holy Spirit. They relinquish the authority of their lives over to him thus making Jesus the Lord of their life as well as Savior. They put their trust in what Jesus accomplished for them when He died, was buried and rose again from the dead (see John 1:12; 14:17,23; 15:4; Rom. 8:11; Rev. 3:20).

Baptism in the Holy Spirit: Given at Pentecost, it is the promise of the Father, sent by Jesus after His ascension, to empower the Church to preach the gospel throughout the whole earth (see Joel 2:28,29; Matt. 3:11; Mark 16:17; Acts 1:5; 2:1-4,17,38,39; 8:14-17; 10:38,44-47; 11:15-17; 19:1-6).

The Gifts of the Holy Spirit: The Holy Spirit is manifested through a variety of spiritual gifts to build and sanctify the church, demonstrate the validity of the resurrection and confirm the power of the Gospel. The Bible lists of these gifts are not necessarily exhaustive, and the gifts may occur in various combinations. All believers are commanded to earnestly desire the manifestation of the gifts in their lives. These gifts always operate in harmony with the Scriptures and should never be used in violation of biblical parameters. (See Heb. 2:4; Rom. 1:11; 12:4-8; Eph. 4:16; 2 Tim. 1:5,16; 4:14; 1 Cor. 12:1-31; 14:1-40; 1 Peter 4:10.)

The Church: The Church is the Body of Christ, the habitation of God through the Spirit, with divine appointments for the fulfillment of Jesus' Great Commission. Every person who is born of the Spirit is an integral part of the Church as a member of the body of believers. There is a spiritual unity of all believers in our Lord Jesus Christ. (See Eph. 1:22; 2:19-22; Heb. 12:23; John 17:11,20-23.)

Two Sacraments

Water Baptism: Following faith in the Lord Jesus Christ, the new convert is commanded by the Word of God to be baptized in water in the name of the Father and of the Son and of the Holy Spirit (see Matt. 28:19; Acts 2:38).

The Lord's Supper: A unique time of Communion in the presence of God when the elements of bread and grape juice (the body and blood of the Lord Jesus Christ) are taken in remembrance of Jesus' sacrifice on the cross. (See Matt. 26:26-29; Mark 16:16; Acts 8:12,36-38; 10:47,48; 1 Cor. 10:16; 11:23-25.)

Healing of the Sick: Healing of the sick is illustrated in the life and ministry of Jesus, and included in the commission of Jesus to His disciples. It is given as a sign which is to follow believers. It is also a part of Jesus' work on the cross and one of the gifts of the Spirit. (See Ps. 103:2,3; Isa. 53:5; Matt. 8:16,17; Mark 16:17,18; Acts 8:6,7; James 5:14-16; 1 Cor. 12:9,28; Rom. 11:29.)

God's Will for Provision: It is the Father's will for believers to become whole, healthy and successful in all areas of life. But because of the Fall, many may not receive the full benefits of God's will while on the earth. That fact, though, should never prevent all believers from seeking the full benefits of Christ's provision in order to better serve others.

- Spiritual (see John 3:3-11; 2 Cor. 5:17-21; Rom. 10:9,10).
- Mental and Emotional (see 2 Tim. 1:7; 2:11; Phil. 4:7,8; Rom. 12:2; Isa. 26:3).
- Physical (see Isa. 53:4,5; Matt. 8:17; 1 Peter 2:24).
- Financial (see Joshua 1:8; Mal. 3:10,11; Luke 6:38; 2 Cor. 9:6-10; Deut. 28:1-14; Ps. 34:10; 84:11; Phil. 4:19).

Resurrection: Jesus Christ was physically resurrected from the dead in a glorified body three days after His death on the cross. In addition, both the saved and the lost will be resurrected; they that are saved to the resurrection of life and they that are lost to the resurrection of eternal damnation (see Luke 24:16,36,39; John 2:19-21; 20:26-28; 21:4; Acts 24:15; 1 Cor. 15:42,44; Phil. 1:21-23; 3:21).

Heaven: Heaven is the eternal dwelling place for all believers in the gospel of Jesus Christ (see Matt. 5:3,12,20; 6:20; 19:21; 25:34; John 17:24; 2 Cor. 5:1; Heb. 11:16; 1 Peter 1:4).

Hell: After living one life on earth, the unbelievers will be judged by God and sent to hell where they will be eternally tormented with the devil and the fallen angels (see Matt. 25:41; Mark 9:43-48; Heb. 9:27; Rev. 14:9-11; 20:12-15; 21:8).

Second Coming: Jesus Christ will physically and visibly return to earth for the second time to establish His kingdom. This will occur at a date undisclosed by the Scriptures (see Matt. 24:30; 26:63-64; Acts 1:9-11; 1 Thess. 4:15-17; 2 Thess. 1:7,8; Rev. 1:7).

---

3. The statement of faith should say exactly what you want the church to believe throughout the generations. Your statement of faith is the way to

protect the church, because no Senior Pastor can ever serve the church who does not believe and teach the creed of the church. To violate the creed is reason for dismissal.

4. We have chosen not to fight over our baptism formula. Matthew 28:19 says, "Therefore go and make disciples of all nations, baptizing them in the name of the Father and the Son and the Holy Spirit." Acts 2:38 says, "Peter replied, 'Repent, and let every one of you be baptized in the name of Jesus Christ for the remission of sins; and you shall receive the gift of the Holy Spirit.'" So when we water baptize, we say something like, "I baptize you in the name of the Father, the Son and the Holy Spirit, in the powerful name of Jesus." This way, all of the biblical references are clearly obeyed.

ARTICLE FOUR

Government[5]

New Life Church is governed by its Congregation, the Trustees of the Corporation, the office of the Senior Pastor and the Overseers. The Congregation determines the spiritual tone, strength and direction of the church by wisely selecting the Senior Pastor (Article 5). The Trustees are to serve the church by setting policy in the management of the church Corporation and making the major financial decisions for the church (Article 6). The Senior Pastor's office is responsible to oversee the day-to-day ministry of the church (Article 7), and the Board of Overseers are to protect the church through counsel and prayer, and, if required, the discipline of the Senior Pastor (Article 8).

5. This article formally introduces the balanced combination of the four primary methods of church government. All churches use these basic systems to one degree or another, but we use each of these in their most positive function, resulting in an excellent separation of power and clearly defined roles.

ARTICLE FIVE

Congregation[6]

Section 1. General Authority to Select a New Senior Pastor.

In the event that a new Senior Pastor is needed by the church, two methods are provided for the Congregational selection of a new Senior Pastor. One method involves the participation of the departing Pastor and the other does not. The founding Pastor of the church does not need to be officially confirmed by the Congregation which is added to him; therefore, he is exempted from Article 5.

Section 2. Congregational Process with the Participation of the Departing Pastor.[7]

(Para. 1) Departing Pastor Participates in Replacement

If the Senior Pastor is in good standing with the church and is removing himself because of retirement or relocation, the following is the selection process:

(Para. 2) Congregational Vote

The Senior Pastor may choose up to two candidates. The first candidate is to speak in three or more of the primary services of the church. Then the Senior Pastor is to formally recommend this candidate in a Monday night meeting of the membership. For any meeting of the membership for pastoral selection, members are to bring their contribution records from the previous year and display them at the door to verify membership. At that meeting, the departing Senior Pastor and the candidate are to leave. Then the Secretary/Treasurer is to conduct a secret ballot vote, and, with a minimum two-thirds (2/3) vote of those members present, the candidate shall be accepted. If that ballot fails, the second candidate which the Senior Pastor has chosen is afforded the same opportunity as the first. If that ballot fails, the process outlined in Section 3 shall be followed.

Section 3. Congregational Process Without Departing Pastor's Participation.[8]

(Para. 1) Departing Pastor Unavailable

If the Senior Pastor is removed by the Overseers, is deceased, cannot or will not participate in the selection process of the new Senior Pastor for any reason, the following shall be the process for selecting a new Senior Pastor:

(Para. 2) Meeting of the Membership

The Secretary/Treasurer or another person appointed by the Board of Trustees is to immediately call a meeting of the membership by making an announcement during the primary Sunday church service. The meeting is to be held in the church building eight days following on a Monday night. At the meeting of the membership, a Pastoral Selection Committee of nine people will be elected by the membership, to include three men and three women from the general membership and the three most senior full-time pastoral staff members. If there are not three full-time pastoral staff members, the membership may elect for those positions people who are familiar with the day-to-day work of the church. The committee itself is to vote and select a chairperson and co-chairperson. The Congregation may elect additional staff members to the Pastoral Selection Committee to fill slots designated for the general membership if it chooses.

(Para. 3) Formation of Pastoral Selection Committee

It is the duty of the Pastoral Selection Committee to provide an interim Pastor or speaker(s) to conduct church services. However, neither an interim Pastor nor any guest speaker shall have the corporate powers of the President.

(Para. 4) Congregational Vote

The committee is to recommend a new Senior Pastor as soon as an acceptable candidate is available. That person must be a licensed or ordained minister of the gospel, and they must be approved by three of the five members of the Board of Overseers before being presented to the church. Once the committee recommends a Senior Pastor candidate, that person may speak to the church in every service for three weeks, after which time a meeting of the membership shall be publicly called on a Monday night, chaired by the Secretary/Treasurer or by a member of the Board of Trustees selected by that Board. At that meeting church members shall vote by secret ballot either to accept or to reject the pastoral candidate. Trustees and their wives are to count the ballots. A minimum two-thirds (2/3) vote of those attending the meeting is required to elect the next Senior Pastor. If there is not a two-thirds (2/3) majority in favor of the candidate, the Pastoral Selection Committee shall seek another candidate.

(Para. 5) Staff Administration During Transition[9]

During the selection process, members of the church staff are to continue in their positions. Should staff or financial problems arise, the Secretary/Treasurer has authority to alter the roles of staff members, including dismissal if necessary in their own judgment. Once the new Senior Pastor is in place, he has full authority to select his own staff, replacing existing staff members, if he should choose, according to the severance agreements (Art. 7, Sec. 2, Par. 5).

6. This section allows Congregational government in the selection of a new Senior Pastor. This process is vitally important in light of the great freedoms the Senior Pastor is given under these bylaws. Those freedoms are necessary for effective and powerful leadership, which places a great deal of responsibility on the people who select him. Remember, once the Senior Pastor is selected, he will direct the spiritual countenance of the entire church for potentially many, many years.

   Don't rush the process. The easiest way to fire someone is to never hire him. And, with this form of government, the person cannot be fired unless a serious offense has been committed. And even then, the Overseers are the only people who can dismiss him. So be wise.

   Because of its importance, this selection process has two parts explained in Sections 2 and 3.

7. This process is to be used if the current Senior Pastor is leaving in good standing. That means he is trusted and respected, and therefore should be fully involved in the appointment of the person who will succeed him.

8. This process is more cumbersome than the first because it provides for the situation where the most recent Senior Pastor is not present due to death, dismissal or a resignation when the Pastor chooses not to participate. The goal is to select God's man as the Senior Pastor. Don't become sidetracked by the process. Always remember the goal.

9. It is proper and right for employees hired by the previous Senior Pastor to make themselves available for resignation any time within a two-year window of the new Senior Pastor's placement. The new Senior Pastor should have the freedom to replace past employees at will during his first two years. This courtesy by the employees is a great contribution to the continued health of the church.

ARTICLE SIX

Trustees of the Corporation[10]

Section 1. General Powers.

The major financial affairs of the Corporation shall be managed by the Board of Trustees, hereinafter referred to as the Trustees, whose members shall have a fiduciary obligation to the Corporation according to Sections 2 and 3 of this Article.

Section 2. Functions.[11]

(Para. 1) Provide Facilities

The Trustees vote in accordance with these Bylaws in order to conduct the major business decisions of the Corporation. The Trustees oversee the provision of the physical facilities needed by the church body. They also coordinate any construction projects which require a loan.

(Para. 2) Exclusive Authority

The Trustees are the only body within the Corporation or church body with the authority (1) to buy and sell real estate, (2) to borrow money or (3) to secure real estate leases.

(Para. 3) Counsel[12]

The Trustees are to provide counsel to the Senior Pastor regarding the major financial affairs of the church.

(Para. 4) Staff Loans

Any employee of the church requesting financial assistance from the church in the form of a loan must first get permission from the Senior Pastor to apply for the loan. The Trustees shall then review the application. All terms and conditions of the loan must be approved by a majority (four or more) of the Trustees.

No loans shall be made to any Officer or Trustee of the Corporation.

Section 3. Financial Guidelines.[13]

(Para. 1) Monies Available to Trustees

In order to provide for the physical needs of the church, the Trustees have available to them 100 percent of all unrestricted monies accumulated in any type of savings accounts (including stocks, bonds, CDs, mutual funds, etc.) and all assets in land and property. In addition, the Trustees may direct any expenditures up to 35 percent of the unrestricted income of the church from tithes, offerings, interest and investments. Current undesignated income is to be determined by the undesignated income of the previous year. From the 35 percent of church income at the Trustees' disposal, payment must be made on all debts and real estate leases of the Corporation.

(Para. 2) Debt Restrictions[14]

Before the Trustees may authorize the church to borrow money or incur a lease obligation, the following conditions must first be met:

1. *Minimum 25 percent down.* Should the Trustees choose to borrow money to facilitate the growth and/or work of the church, it must first accumulate 25 percent of the total price of the project for a down payment in determining whether sufficient funds have been accumulated, either (1) amounts previously expended on the project to be financed from the proceeds of such indebtedness will be deemed accumulated, or (2) amounts previously expended as principle reduction payments above minimum required payments on preexisting loans during the 24 months prior to incur-

ring additional debt will be deemed accumulated and credited toward the 25 percent.

2. *Maximum 35 percent payment ceiling.* The combined totals of all monthly debt service and real estate lease payments, following the incurring of the indebtedness or lease obligation under consideration, will not exceed 35 percent of the average monthly total income. The percentage shall be based on, but not be limited to, tithes, offerings, investment income and unrestricted gifts of the church.

3. *Lease to purchase allowance.* If indebtedness is being secured to build a structure that will relieve the church of its need for a leased facility that will be vacated when the new building is completed, then the current lease commitment need not be calculated into the 35 percent expenditure limitation for 18 months. Thus, the church is allowed 18 months for both construction and lease payments that, combined, exceed the 35 percent limit, only if there is compelling assurance that by the end of the 18-month period it is reasonable to expect relief from the burden of the lease payment.

4. *Income projections.* The church may not set budgets, meet conditions for borrowing or make any financial commitments based on upward projections of income.

5. *Audit requirements.* If the church wishes to borrow over $250,000, the Trustees must base its financial limitations on information provided by an audit of the previous year.

6. *Church plant exception.* If the church has less than 12 months' financial history and wishes to borrow less

than $250,000, that decision may be based on the most current three months of financial history provided by the church Treasurer. Even in this situation, the 25 percent down and 35 percent debt service ceilings must be met.

(Para. 3) Annual Audit

If the income of the church exceeds $250,000 per year, the Trustees shall obtain an annual audit performed by an independent public accounting firm in accordance with Generally Accepted Auditing Standards (GAAS), with financial statements prepared in accordance with Generally Accepted Accounting Principles (GAAP).

(Para. 4) Audit Review Committee

The Trustees shall appoint the Secretary/Treasurer and two other members of the Trustee Board to serve as an audit review committee. After reviewing the annual audit, they are to report their findings at a Trustees meeting.

(Para. 5) Conflict of Interest

In order to avoid any conflict of interest, all of the following criteria must be met for any business transaction to be made between a Trustee and the Corporation:

1. The Trustee with whom the transaction is being considered is excluded from any discussions for approving the transaction.
2. The Trustees consider competitive bids or comparable valuations.
3. The Trustees act upon and demonstrate that the transaction is in the best interest of the Corporation.

4. The transaction must be fully disclosed in the end-of-year audited financial statements of the Corporation.

Section 4. Appointment, Number, Term and Qualifications.[15]

(Para. 1) Number and Selection

The Trustees shall be composed of seven members, who are appointed by the Senior Pastor and approved by the Board of Elders. Trustees may not be employees or staff members of the Corporation, nor can they be related by blood or marriage to employees or staff members. All pastoral appointments to the Board of Trustees must be approved by the Board of Elders (Article 9). The term of office for each Trustee shall continue until such Trustee resigns from office or from membership in the church, dies or is removed. All Trustees must be selected from the membership of the church.

(Para. 2) Removal

The Pastor may dismiss Trustees without cause, but at a rate that does not exceed one dismissal every six months. The Elders are not required to approve pastoral dismissals of Trustees. In the event that the office of Pastor is vacant, the Secretary/Treasurer may appoint or dismiss Trustees subject to the same limitations that apply to appointments and dismissals by the Senior Pastor in accordance with this paragraph and Article 6, Section 4, Para. 1.

(Para. 3) Exclusive Role

Because the Trustees are responsible for the major financial decisions of the church, they must resign their position on the Board if they ever become a staff member or take any other paid position within the church. Volunteer work within the church is encouraged, but paid positions may constitute a conflict of interest.

Section 5. Meetings.[16]

(Para. 1) Frequency of Meetings

A meeting of the Trustees shall be held at least twice a year. The Senior Pastor, or any Trustee, may call a meeting at any time, under the condition that a majority (four or more) of the Trustees attend the meeting.

(Para. 2) Leadership of Meetings

If at all possible, the Pastor is to attend and lead each Trustees meeting. If not possible, the Secretary/Treasurer shall lead the meeting. If neither the Pastor nor the Secretary/Treasurer is able to lead the meeting, the Trustees must choose a leader for that meeting and proceed in order, with the appointed leader keeping minutes for the record. Any motions passed and recorded in a meeting without the Pastor or the Secretary/Treasurer may not take effect until the following meeting with either the Pastor or the Secretary/Treasurer present when the minutes of the previous meeting are approved.

(Para. 3) Location of Meetings

Any meeting of the Trustees may be held at such place or places as shall from time to time be determined by the Trustees or fixed by the Senior Pastor and designated in the notice of the meeting.

(Para. 4) Written Notice of Meetings

Whenever, under the provisions of a statute or the Articles of Incorporation or these bylaws, a written notice is required to be given to any Trustee: (1) such notice may be given in writing by fax or by mail at such fax number or address as appears on the books of the Corporation and such notice shall be deemed to be given at the time the notice is faxed or mailed; (2) the person entitled to such notice may waive the notice by signing a written waiver either before, at or after the time of the meeting; and (3) the appearance of such person or persons at the meeting shall be equivalent to signing a written waiver of notice.

(Para. 5) Regular Meetings

The Trustees may establish regular meetings. No notice shall be required for any regular meeting.

(Para. 6) Trustee Action Without Meeting

Any action which may be taken at a meeting of the Trustees may be taken without a meeting if a consent in writing setting forth the action taken is signed by all the Trustees and such action shall be effective as of the date specified in the written consent.

(Para. 7) Teleconferencing

At any meeting of the Trustees, any person may participate in the meeting by telephone provided all members of the Trustees present at the meeting or by telephone can hear and speak to each other. Participation by telephone shall be equivalent to attending the meeting in person.

(Para. 8) Quorum

A majority (four or more) of the Trustees shall constitute a quorum for the transaction of business at any meeting. The act of a majority of the Trustees shall be the act of the Board of Trustees. In the absence of a quorum at any meeting, a meeting of the Trustees present may adjourn the meeting without further notice until a quorum shall be established.

Section 6. Compensation.

Trustees, as such, shall not receive any salaries for their services.

10. This section clarifies that the Board has the fiduciary responsibility for the Corporation.
11. This section explains roles that only the Board of Trustees can fulfill. Most churches could have avoided problems over the exercise of authority if this section had been in their bylaws. This section firmly establishes the corporate Board to take action once the spiritual Body has demonstrated financial strength. This section is a great protection for the Senior Pastor and the church body at large.
12. Counsel for the Senior Pastor can be interpreted as pressure. Therefore, the Trustees are responsible for discussing with the Senior Pastor items helpful to his decision-making processes. I talk regularly with Board members in stand-up meetings before or after a church service, discussing different issues. This does not require the Board meeting format or setting. Because different members on the Board have different areas of expertise, I casually talk with our Trustees when I see them at the church to get input. This is always helpful.
13. This section provides the framework the Trustees can use to serve the church. It is a provision to keep anyone from placing too much money in buildings and not enough in direct ministry toward people. All monies saved, and up to 35 percent of the income of the church, can be used by the Trustees, but the amount cannot exceed these limits. The limitation is a protection for the ministry aspects of the church. People love knowing that their tithes and offerings are going to ministry, not just buildings, and that even in times of expansion, no more than 35 percent of their tithes and offerings to the church go toward construction and debt service. This provision is a great motivator for the people in their giving. And it does allow

the Pastor to choose to save as much as he would like toward a project. The limitation is only on indebtedness, not savings.

14. This section including its six subparagraphs keeps the church from incurring too much debt. It requires past performance before borrowing. Really, it keeps the church from making a financial mistake based on a dream, speculation or what people perceive as God's direction. These requirements do not unduly restrict, but provide a realistic constraint from overly aggressive financial commitments. With the 25 percent minimum down, 35 percent limit on payments, the Congregation is secure and the business people will perceive the church as wise and conservative. This plan works well for all.

15. Some complain that in a beginning church, it is impossible to have seven people who could fulfill the role of a Trustee Board. If that is the case, you might not be ready to have a church structure. (Some rural communities would be one exception.) Maybe a Bible study format would be adequate with a club account at the bank. Then, when your group has grown to the point that seven people could fill Trustee positions, incorporate and begin the actual process of establishing a working church structure.

Remember that this Board is not an Elder Board or a deacon Board, so these people do not have to meet the biblical requirements for spiritual leadership in the church. This is a business Board. Choose people who have a steady, consistent walk with Christ and long-lasting, positive relationships and are financially responsible. Select people who have proven themselves responsible in other, natural areas of life. If a person wants authority or says he/she would like to be a Trustee, respectfully decline. Watch out for subtle forms of pseudo-submission to win your favor. Choose people who are genuine servants and love God. They will always be a blessing. Lastly, make sure they love you so they will utilize the Corporation to serve the body of believers in a way that glorifies God.

Balance is achieved through the Pastor's responsibility to appoint Trustees. Should a Pastor, however, want to change the Board too quickly, he is limited in that he can only appoint and dismiss one Trustee every six months. This stipulation protects everyone and leaves proper balance of power in case of difficulty. Provision is also made here should the Pastor no longer be with the church. In that case, the Overseers can appoint or dismiss Trustees, keeping the church functional for a long interval without a Pastor.

16. Don't have unnecessary meetings. If the church is building or moving, meet once a month. We meet on the second Sunday afternoon of every month at 4:00 P.M. when there is business. If not, we meet at the beginning of the year to review audit reports and in the fall for an update. That's all that needs to be done unless money is being borrowed, land purchased or buildings being built. Keep it simple.

ARTICLE SEVEN

Senior Pastor of the Church/President of the Corporation[17]

Section 1. The Office of the Senior Pastor.

(Para. 1) Dual Role of the Senior Pastor

Because New Life Church has two complimentary branches, the spiritual body of believers and the legal Corporation, it is the Senior Pastor who administratively bridges the gap between the two branches. Even though the dual roles are sometimes awkward, because the Senior Pastor is primarily responsible for the spiritual life of the church, the Pastor must be in a position corporately to ensure that financial strength is directed toward the ministries of his choice.

(Para. 2) Responsibilities of the Senior Pastor

It is the Pastor's responsibility to:
- Provide biblical vision and direction for the Congregation,
- Define and communicate the church's purpose,
- Oversee and coordinate the day-to-day ministry of the Congregation and administration of the church,
- Appoint a Board of Overseers pursuant to Article 8,
- Recognize and enlist apostolic, prophetic, evangelistic, pastoral and teaching ministries, along with that of Elders, Deacons, and additional staff members as he deems biblical and necessary for the healthy and balanced spiritual ministry to the body of believers,
- Select Trustees pursuant to Article 6 who will help oversee the business of the Corporation,

- Staff the church as he deems necessary to help administrate the affairs of the Corporation,
- Veto any nominations to the Board of Elders pursuant to Article 9.

(Para. 3) The Pastor's Spiritual Leadership

In his role as Senior Pastor, he may work with Overseers, Elders, Deacons or anyone serving in any fivefold ministry offices as outlined in Ephesians 4:11-13 in any way that he determines is biblical. In addition, he may budget monies, hire staff, develop projects or ministry, and create cell groups or other specialized ministries according to his convictions and biblical understanding. He shall have the authority to appoint and approve any assistants that are necessary to properly carry on the work of the church.

(Para. 4) The Pastor's Responsibility for Services

Times, order of services and the leadership of services are to be determined by him or by the spiritual church structure that he establishes. No person shall be invited to speak, teach or minister at a service held in church-owned facilities, or in the name of the church, without the approval of the Pastor or the appropriate member of the established church ministry team.

Section 2. The Office of the President.[18]

(Para.1) The President

The Corporation finds its headship under the Lord Jesus Christ and in its President. The Senior Pastor shall serve as the President and Chief Executive Officer of the Corporation. If possible, he shall preside at all meetings of the Board of Trustees and shall see that all orders and resolutions of the Board are put into effect. He shall execute in the name of the Corporation all deeds, bonds, mortgages, contracts and other documents authorized by the Board of Trustees. He shall be an ex-officio member of all standing committees, and shall have the general powers and duties of supervision and management usually vested in the office of the President of a Corporation.

(Para. 2) The President's Role with Trustees

The President is the non-voting chairman of the Board of Trustees. He calls meetings and determines the agenda in consultation with the Trustees. The President shall make selections to the Board of Trustees from the church membership at a rate not to exceed one new appointment every six months in accordance with Article 6. The President may also dismiss Trustees, but at a rate that does not exceed one dismissal every six months in accordance with Article 6, Section 4, Paragraph 2.

(Para. 3) The President's Role in Administration[19]

The President is the senior administrator of the church. He is ultimately responsible for all day-to-day administrative decisions of the church.

(Para. 4) The President's Role with Staff[20]

The President hires, directs and dismisses staff. As the Senior Pastor, his call is confirmed to the church through the Congregation, and those hired through him are to assist him in fulfilling this calling.

(Para. 5) The President's Role in Establishing Salaries

The President determines all salaries and writes pay scales for full-time salaried employees. Pay scales shall be explained to new full-time salaried employees and, should they ever be changed, they will be given in writing to the affected employees. If there is a severance pay agreement, that too must be given to the employee in writing. In addition, all part-time salaries and hourly wages are variable and are to be determined between the President and the employee.

(Para. 6) The President's Salary Exceptions[21]

The salary of the President is to be on a pay scale consistent with the pay scale established for the other members of the pastoral team with two exceptions. These are:

(1) *Housing:* The President (Senior Pastor) may live in a parsonage owned and maintained by the Corporation. The parsonage shall be chosen by the Board of Trustees.

(2) *Transportation:* The Senior Pastor shall be provided with two automobiles, which will be maintained by the Corporation. The cost of the automobiles shall be determined by the Trustees. The Corporation shall then purchase or lease the vehicle of the Pastor's choice within the budget allowed. Each automobile is to be kept for six years. During his first three years of service at the church, only one automobile shall be provided; then, at the beginning of the fourth year, the second shall be purchased or leased. Henceforth, a new vehicle is to be purchased or

leased every three years. Should the President choose to replace a vehicle before six years expires, the value remaining in the previous vehicle is the maximum that may be spent. The President, though, may contribute personal funds toward the purchase of the replacement vehicle. No additional funds may be added by the Corporation for the purchase of a vehicle out of sequence.

(Para. 7) Optional Benefits

After the Senior Pastor has served for a minimum of 10 consecutive years, the Trustees may provide additional benefits which are unique to the Senior Pastor position. They may, for example, choose to provide an additional retirement benefit in order to compensate for the fact that the Senior Pastor is unable to build equity in a home while living in a church-owned parsonage. They may also choose to reduce the amount of time the Senior Pastor is required to keep a vehicle before it is replaced. These benefits or any others like them must be initiated by the Trustees and not the Senior Pastor because these benefits are optional and not required to be provided. They are purely an attempt to reward many years of faithful service.

(Para. 8) Budget[22]

After the church is one year old, an annual budget must be prepared. The budget is to be based on 90 percent of the previous year's undesignated income. The President is to write the budget for 65 percent of the 90 percent in order to finance the basic ministry needs of the church (salaries, taxes, bills, missions, benevolence, department financial allocations, etc.). He is free to reflect his values and wisdom in his budget portion. Then, the President is to work with the Trustees to add their 35 percent to the budget.

(Para. 9) Expenditures

Budgeted amounts are not to be considered actual monies available. Nothing can be spent by the President except actual funds that are available, and those monies are to be spent according to the budget. The President may not borrow money, sign leases, buy or sell real estate or make any agreements that could force indebtedness upon the church. Should the church borrow, the Trustees may give the President authority to spend those monies on the project for which the funds were borrowed. All undesignated monies that are available to the Corporation above budgeted amounts are deemed discretionary and are available to be spent by the President, but he may only obligate funds currently on hand.

17. This section emphasizes the Senior Pastor's role as the spiritual leader of the local church. It distinguishes the two branches that must work in harmony—the Corporation and the spiritual Body. Then it clarifies that (a) the Corporation exists to serve the spiritual Body, and (b) that the Senior Pastor is responsible for leading the spiritual Body and using his influence to cause the corporate structure to serve that Body. So Section 1 emphasizes the role of Senior Pastor, and Section 2 explains the Senior Pastor's role as President of the Corporation.

18. The distinct role as President in contrast to Pastor is significant. Remember that churches worship God, communicate the Word, pray for people, minister the life of the Holy Spirit to others and foster additional ministry. Corporations, on the other hand, hire and fire people, pay taxes, process money, buy and sell buildings, accumulate assets, etc. These two roles are distinctly different, but they overlap in every ministry. These bylaws distinguish the two roles. And, as you can see, the corporate roles, when implemented with simplicity, facilitate ministry. The Corporation, though, is not the purpose of the organization—the spiritual Body is.

So this section explains the corporate role of the Senior Pastor. As we have already seen, the Trustees make the major financial decisions for the church. But in Paragraph 2, we notice that the Pastor nominates Trustees, the Elders approve the nominations, and, if necessary, the Pastor removes Trustees. But the Pastor cannot dismiss Trustees at a rate faster than one every six months. This provision is needed in case the Pastor's heart becomes sinful and he wants to "stack the Board." Also, if the Pastor has a conflict with the Trustees, he can't do too much too quickly—thus, everyone is protected. Remember, we want churches that remain strong and healthy for years—generations. So, the Senior Pastor can change the Board, but not too fast. With this time delay, it would take three and a half years to change the entire Board—enough time for the condition of heart to become evident to all. At the same time, should a Trustee's heart become sinful, the Senior Pastor has the authority to remove that person quickly.

19. This paragraph clarifies that the Senior Pastor is the senior administrator. When a church is small, the Pastor himself will often have to do all of the administration. When a church becomes large enough to afford it, a full-time administrator should be hired to serve the day-to-day ministries of the church and report directly to the Senior Pastor.

20. Paragraphs 4 and 5 clarify that the Senior Pastor, unless he is the founding Pastor, is selected by the Congregation, but all other staff members are hired by the Senior Pastor to help him serve. Therefore, according to these bylaws, the Senior Pastor is ultimately accountable to the Board of Overseers while the rest of the staff is ultimately accountable to the Senior Pastor.

"I work for the church, and the staff works for me." This causes the staff to work together in great harmony and prevents unnecessary problems with staff members who might become disgruntled and try to undermine the Senior Pastor.

The ability of the Senior Pastor to set salaries is vitally important. Many church systems allow the Pastor to set salaries for everyone but himself, and allow a governing Board to set the Pastor's salary. Not good. This could imply that the Senior Pastor works for a church Board. He does not. The Trustees already determine the home and the value of the automobiles the church will provide for the Senior Pastor and his family. The same problem exists if the Congregation sets pastoral salaries. The implication is that the Senior Pastor is an employee who can be hired or fired by anyone other than the Board of Overseers.

Most churches have four primary classifications of workers: (1) pastoral staff (2) salaried support staff (3) hourly support staff and (4) volunteers. The Senior Pastor must design a universal pay scale for the pastoral staff. This way he knows that his base pay, experience-credit ratio and dependent allowance will be the same as the other Pastors. Therefore, if he wants to pay himself a certain amount, the other Pastors will need to be paid on the same scale. (Two exceptions do exist, and we will discuss them in detail later.) This provision creates a beautiful balance, and greatly reduces any sense of unfairness in pay among the pastoral team.

Our universal pay scale has evolved throughout the years, and you may be able to develop a better one than ours. But currently, our pay scale for pastoral staff starts with a $2,300-per-month base. To that base we give credit for work experience at a ratio of three to one. For every three years of experience, we give a 10 percent compounded raise. This must be experience that has helped train for the current position and does not include years in school. Thus, if someone had 12 years of qualified experience, we would give that person 4 years credit. Compounded at 10 percent a year, this would equal an additional $1,067 per month. We also give a $65-per-month allowance for every dependent. So if the Pastor is married with two children, another $195 per month would be added. In this example, the Pastor's gross monthly salary would be $3,367. This figure includes the Pastor's housing allowance, which is nontaxable. In addition to salaries, the Pastors are provided family medical insurance, retirement benefits and paid vacation. Even though this isn't an official agreement, we give at least a 10 percent raise to everyone if the church has grown 10 percent or more, which means that every person who has ever worked at New Life has received at least a 10 percent raise every year for 13 years now.

If this pay package is not enough, it is increased for all the pastoral staff. If the Senior Pastor can't live on the allotted amount, then the youth Pastor can't either. This system has remarkable secondary benefits to the entire staff and church. For those who use it, it works very well.

Everyone would agree that the Senior Pastor is worthy of his hire because of his calling. Why, then, would we think a youth Pastor or an administrative Pastor should be paid less? If these Pastors are fulfilling their callings, and God has placed them in their positions, shouldn't they also be compensated appropriately? How many youth Pastors have had to become Senior Pastors because as their families grew, they needed to increase the family income? What a crime. Who would dare say the Senior Pastor works harder or longer hours than the youth Pastor? No one who has been one.

The primary differential for income among the Pastors should be in regard to tenure. If a Pastor serves in a church for a longer period of time, that Pastor will know more people have more proven worth of influence in more people's lives. His pay, therefore, should be raised to reflect his extended time of service. Not everyone at New Life makes the same, but all Pastors are paid from the same scale.

21. The following exceptions are the only differences between the associate pastoral staff and the Senior Pastor, with the reasoning that the Senior Pastor holds corporate and spiritual responsibilities. The associate Pastor and the support staff work exclusively under the Senior Pastor. The values

of these extra benefits, though, are solely at the discretion of the Trustees and outside the direct control of the Senior Pastor.

The two exceptions to the pay-scale system are clearly stated in Paragraph 6. Note, though, the balance in selecting the house and the vehicle(s). The Trustees select the house the church will provide, so regardless of church size, if the church hires a full-time Pastor, it can determine the value of the housing for the Pastor and his family. In addition, the Trustees determine the value of the cars the Pastor receives.

If a car is wrecked during the six years, the Pastor may use the remaining value in the car to replace it from insurance. These two paragraphs are very sensitive and, of course may be changed. Some Pastors already have their own homes, others prefer driving their own cars. In those cases, adjustments need to be made in this provision. For example, the Trustees may choose to allow the Pastor to use the financial allowance to increase his retirement. Whatever the case, make sure the Senior Pastor is on the same pay scale as other Pastors, and that these two exceptions are not stumbling blocks.

People on the support staff are also fulfilling God's call by serving throughout the church. Support-staff pay scales are set according to job classifications, experience, responsibility, performance, etc. All of our pay rates are fair and in compliance with good stewardship of the tithes and offerings entrusted to us.

The view we hold regarding wage is this: It is impossible to place a value on a calling. We could never afford to pay people what they are worth. So, paychecks are given to our staff out of the tithes and offerings to enable their ministries. If the church did not pay the staff, these people would have to work elsewhere to earn a living. This would greatly affect the amount of time and energy they would have available to answer their calls to ministry. Therefore, our wages are a gift, not compensation for services rendered. Hopefully, all of our staff believes so much in their callings that if it were impossible for the church to pay them, they would find a way to make a living and still dedicate themselves to fulfill their callings through the church.

That brings us to volunteers. Without volunteers we could not continue to minister as effectively as we do. The fact that volunteers don't get paid does not mean they are not called. On the contrary: Volunteers themselves have clearly settled in their hearts that what they are doing is not a job. There is no hireling mentality among volunteers.

Volunteers are as much a part of the team as any paid staff member and should be treated with respect. Volunteers must be screened as carefully as staff members. You don't want to discourage good people, but trouble can occur when the volunteer process is too loose. Whether paid or not, you want the people God has called and added to your ministry team.

22. This paragraph is packed full of philosophical positions we believe are vital

to protect good Christian people from overzealous leadership. Note: Budgets are prepared on 90 percent of the previous year's unrestricted income. Why? So believers won't be constantly pressured by the church leadership to come up with extra money to meet a budget.

ARTICLE EIGHT

Overseers[23]

(Para. 1) New Life Church Requirements to be an Overseer

The members of the Board of Overseers must be active Senior Pastors of respected Congregations who know and love New Life Church and its Senior Pastor or be ministers known for apostolic wisdom and authority. They must agree to make themselves available at their own expense to serve New Life Church if requested by the Elders (Article 13, Section 2), and must be willing to provide spiritual protection to the church through prayer and by living an honorable Christian lifestyle.

(Para. 2) Biblical Qualifications for Overseers

"Now the overseer must be above reproach, the husband of but one wife, temperate, self-controlled, respectable, hospitable, able to teach, not given to drunkenness, not violent but gentle, not quarrelsome, not a lover of money. He must manage his own family well and see that his children obey him with proper respect. (If anyone does not know how to manage his own family, how can he take care of God's church?) He must not be a recent convert, or he may become conceited and fall under the same judgment as the devil. He must also have a good reputation with outsiders, so that he will not fall into disgrace and into the devil's trap." (1 Timothy 3:2-7)

(Para. 3) Selection and Function of Overseers

A Board of Overseers will be nominated by the Pastor and confirmed by the Elders. The Pastor will be accountable to the Overseers in the event of alleged misconduct in compliance with Article 13.

(Para. 4) Installing new Overseers

Each year the Senior Pastor and the Elders may replace one of the Overseers and enter that change into the minutes of a Trustees meeting. If disciplinary action is being considered, changes in the Board of Overseers may not be made until its work is completed.

23. This provision is unique for independent churches. Here, an outside Board is given authority to discipline the Senior Pastor. These bylaws allow checks and balances to all leadership groups. Additional details are given in Article 9.

ARTICLE NINE

Elders[24]

(Para. 1) Spiritual Role

The Board of Elders are to covenant together with the Congregation and the Senior Pastor for the development of the spiritual life of the church. These men and their spouses are to be the primary protectors and encouragers of a positive spiritual climate within the church body. They are neither a governing nor a corporate Board, but a spiritual Board called to create and maintain stability in potentially negative situations.

(Para. 2) Definition

The Elders are men who function within the local church but are not members of the pastoral staff of the church. They are men who meet the biblical qualifications for eldership and function in that calling, but derive their income from sources other than the church. The number of Elders shall be determined by the Senior Pastor but shall not be less than 12.

(Para. 3) Functions[25]

The functions of the Elders are:

1) Maintain and teach by living a godly, Christian lifestyle.

2) Provide a prayer shield for the pastoral team and the local church.

3) Defend, protect and support the integrity of the pastoral team and the local church.

4) Pray for the sick.

5) Organize, implement and execute licensing and ordination requirements and procedures.

6) Mediate disputes among the brethren.

7) Counsel.

8) Confirm or reject pastoral appointments to the Board of Trustees and the Board of Overseers.

9) Contact the Board of Overseers to initiate investigation and potential discipline of the Senior Pastor.

10) To modify the Statement of Faith.

(Para. 4) Biblical Qualifications for Eldership

"An Elder must be blameless, the husband of but one wife, a man whose children believe and are not open to the charge of being wild and disobedient. Since an overseer is entrusted with God's work, he must be blameless—not overbearing, not quick-tempered, not given to drunkenness, not violent, not pursuing dishonest gain. Rather he must be hospitable, one who loves what is good, who is self-controlled, upright, holy and disciplined. He must hold firmly to the trustworthy message as it has been taught, so that he can encourage others by sound doctrine and refute those who oppose it." (Titus 1:6-9)

(Para. 5) Nomination and Appointment to the Board of Elders[26]

Selection of the Elders will be preceded by the Senior Pastor teaching on the biblical requirements for eldership at a Sunday service. Anonymous nominations for the position of Elder will be made in writing immediately after the sermon on eldership by those present at the service. These nominations will be tallied by the Pastor and his associates, and the Elders will be selected from those with the largest number of nominations. The Senior

Pastor can veto anyone's nomination. This nomination process may occur as often as an Elder's term expires or the Senior Pastor feels it is necessary for new Elders to be added.

(Para. 6) Four-Year Service Terms

Once selected to serve on the Elder Board, the Elder and their spouse are to serve for a maximum of four years. After that time of service, the selection process is to be repeated and anyone renominated and appointed may serve as many times as the Congregation and Pastor choose. However, should the Congregation fail to renominate any certain Elder, the Pastor may not select him for service.

(Para. 7) Removal of an Elder

Should anyone in the Congregation, including a staff member or another Elder, bring accusation against an Elder, charging that he does not qualify for eldership, a seven-member group from the staff and the Elder Board may hear the accusations and any response from the accused Elder. Three are to be chosen by the accused Elder, and four are to be chosen by the Senior Pastor. The Senior Pastor may not serve on the panel judging the Elder, but may oversee the procedures if he chooses. Then, in an anonymous vote, if five or more agree that the Elder does not meet the qualifications of eldership, that Elder may no longer serve on the Elder Board.

(Para. 8) Replacement of Elders

During the four years of service, those Elders who are no longer able to serve for any reason need not be replaced as long as at least 12 Elders remain.

(Para. 9) Statement of Faith

Two-thirds of the serving Elders and the Senior Pastor may amend, modify, add to or delete any portion of Section 3, the Statement of Faith, in the same process described in Article 14.

24. This is the only "Board" that includes the spouses in its function. All Elder meetings and functions should fully include the spouses because of the function they have within the Body. We see the Elders as the keel on the bottom of the boat—keeping it upright in the midst of a storm. We also see the Elders as the primary prayer shield for the church.

25. The 10 functions of the Elders are listed in the bylaws for a specific reason. The Elders do not have the same responsibilities as the Trustees—even though from time to time they may want to—nor do they have the same responsibilities as the Overseers. They are, instead, co-laborers with the Senior Pastor and his staff to fulfill the spiritual direction and calling of the church.

26. This paragraph explains the process for selecting Elders. We think it's best not to announce when this service will take place so lobbying does not occur. You want an honest, impromptu response from the Congregation.

    Here's how to do it: the Senior Pastor should preach about the qualifications for an Elder. Then have the ushers hand out 3x5 cards and ask the Congregation to clearly write the name of one person in the church who most fits the qualifications of an Elder. Read the Bible text one more time while people are thinking and writing. Have the ushers pick up all the cards and give them to a member of the pastoral team.

    At that point, no one knows if they were nominated or how many times. It's important that the Senior Pastor's office tally the nominations confidentially. During the sorting process, some people may need to be disqualified by the pastoral team. Because of the nature of their positions, they will know about some people in the Congregation who will be nominated who, in fact, should not serve as Elders for private reasons. Those facts should not be known to anyone.

    Then you can create a list of potential Elders. Send the select nominees letters explaining that they have been nominated as Elders. Include the scriptural basis for Eldership and delineate the 10 Eldership responsibilities (like a job description). Ask the nominees to evaluate their own lives to see if they think they qualify to serve for a four-year term.

    Should they need to decline, they do not have to give a reason. Should they accept, they should call the office and let you know. That group and their spouses may serve for four years. Schedule a time during a Sunday service to recognize and commission the new Elders and their spouses.

Explain briefly the responsibilities of Elders and have the Congregation pray over them.

We suggest that if an Elder develops difficulties, that person not be removed from office too quickly. There may be exceptions, and thus the provision in Paragraph 7. When Elders face difficulty in their families or personal lives, they will usually resign. However, if the Board is large enough to absorb the temporary unavailability of an Elder(s) working through personal conflict, and the benefits gained will outweigh removing the person(s), it is best to stay in the tree of life in these groups as much as possible. Relax and be full of grace.

ARTICLE TEN[27]

Officers

Section 1. Officers.

The officers of the Corporation shall be a President and a Secretary/Treasurer and any other officers that the Trustees may authorize from time to time.

Section 2. Appointment, Election and Term of Office.

(Para. 1) Appointment of the President

The appointment and responsibilities of the President are listed in Articles 5 and 7 above.

(Para. 2) Appointment of Secretary/Treasurer

The Secretary/Treasurer is to be nominated by the President and approved by the Trustees. The term of this office is indefinite. Should the Trustees fail to approve of the nomination of the President, other nominations must be made until a suitable candidate to the Trustees is nominated. The Secretary/Treasurer may be removed by the President.

(Para. 3) New Offices

New offices may be created and filled at any meeting of the Board of Trustees. Each officer shall hold office until his successor has been duly elected and qualified.

Section 3. Removal of Officers.

(Para. 1) Overseers' Responsibility for the President

The Overseers of the church may discipline or remove the President according to Article 13.

(Para 2) Trustees Responsibility for All Other Officers

Any officer elected or appointed by the Board of Trustees may be removed by the Board whenever in its judgment the best interests of the Corporation would be served thereby, but such removal shall be without prejudice to the contract rights, if any, of the officer so removed.

Section 4. Powers of Officers.

(Para. 1) The President

The powers of the President are listed in Article 7 above.

(Para. 2) The Secretary/Treasurer

The Secretary/Treasurer should be a Trustee as well as an officer of the Corporation. As Secretary, the Secretary/Treasurer shall act as clerk and record (or have recorded) all votes and the minutes of all proceedings in a book to be kept for that purpose. He shall oversee the keeping of the membership rolls of the Corporation, and in general perform the duties usually incident to the office of Secretary, and such further duties as shall be prescribed from time to time by the Board of Trustees or by the President.

(Para. 3) The Secretary/Treasurer's Role over Accounting[28]

As Treasurer, the Secretary/Treasurer shall oversee the keeping of full and accurate accounts of the receipts and disbursements in books belonging to the Corporation, and shall oversee the deposit of all monies and other valuable effects in the name and to the credit of the Corporation in such banks and depositories as may be designated by the President. He does not determine expenditures, but he shall oversee the disbursement of the funds of the Corporation as may be ordered by the Trustees or the President. He shall perform the duties usually incident to the office of Treasurer and such other duties as may be prescribed from time to time by the Board of Trustees or by the President.

(Para. 4) Audited Financial Statements

The Secretary/Treasurer shall serve on the Audit Review Committee and report to the Trustees after its review of the annual audit. If the church does not have an annual audit, the Secretary/Treasurer is to provide to the Board a report on the previous year's income and disbursements.

(Para. 5) Cash Flow Statements[29]

The Secretary/Treasurer is to work with the President to provide an annual cash flow statement that must accompany all giving receipts to members. That report is to include the specific amounts of cash remunerations received from the church to specific pastoral staff members. Benefits, support staff salaries, and other items may be grouped together, but the cash portion of the pastoral pay packages must be itemized individually.

(Para. 6) Public Availability of Annual Financial Statements

The Secretary/Treasurer shall insure that current audited financial statements are available to anyone upon written request and the previous year's cash flow statements are available to all contributors to the church.

Section 5. Trustees' Selection of Additional Officers.[30]

In case of the absence of any officer of the Corporation except the President, or for any other reason that may seem necessary to the Board, the Board of Trustees, by a majority vote, may delegate the duties and powers of that officer for the time being to any other officer, or to any Trustee.

27. In Colorado, the law requires only two officers. Check your own state law to see what is required. Avoid having Vice Presidents, because the implication is that the Vice President will become President should the President no longer be in the church. This is not true. If three offices are required by your state, I suggest appointing a President/Pastor, secretary and treasurer. However, if possible, combine the Secretary/Treasurer position.

The Secretary/Treasurer is appointed by the President and approved by the Board of Trustees. That appointment is permanent unless the person resigns or is removed by the President.

28. There is a subtle safety measure here that some don't catch. The Secretary/Treasurer is responsible to oversee the bookkeeping of the church. The Secretary/ Treasurer is not responsible to determine expendi-

tures, but is responsible to make sure accurate records are being kept and reported. The financial office does our bookkeeping. The financial office works under the Senior Pastor but is also accountable to the Secretary/Treasurer.

Why is that important? Because if the Senior Pastor became dishonest or began to do something unusual with finances, the accounting staff would be responsible to tell him without any fear of recourse. If he did not correct the situation, they would then bring it to the attention of the Secretary/Treasurer. A safety measure such as this protects the Pastor from a greedy, deceptive heart and protects the accounting staff in the midst of a potentially difficult situation. It is very important that someone not paid by the church oversees the financial records. This system works well.

The provision's requirement that the Secretary/Treasurer attend all sessions of the Board of Trustees does not mean the Board cannot meet and do business when the Secretary/Treasurer is absent. It means the Secretary/Treasurer's functions must be performed when the Secretary/Treasurer is absent, and that if the Secretary/Treasurer is in town, every effort must be made on this person's part to attend.

29. This paragraph is vitally important. We believe that everyone who gives to the church should be able to know exactly how much money the church received, how much was spent and for what (i.e., each pastoral staff member's salary on a line-item basis). Believing that the funds given to the church are people's worship to God and knowing that cash flow statements must be mailed out at the end of every year makes those who spend the tithes and offerings much more thoughtful. They know that the missions support, internal payroll, benevolence gifts, operations expenses and other expenditures will be openly accounted for and not "hidden" in a pie chart or percentage graph.

30. Section 5 allows for additional officers. I don't recommend this because I think every circumstance should be covered with the already existing provisions. However, if something unforeseen develops, this provision does allow flexibility.

ARTICLE ELEVEN

Business Practices

Section 1. Fiscal Year.

The fiscal year of the Corporation shall be the calendar year.

Section 2. Contracts.

The Board of Trustees may authorize any officer or officers, agent or agents of the Corporation, in addition to the officers so authorized by these Bylaws, to enter into any contract or execute and deliver any instrument in the name of and on behalf of the Corporation. Such authority may be general or may be confined to specific instances.

Section 3. Checks, Drafts or Orders.

All checks, drafts, orders for the payment of money, notes or other evidences of indebtedness issued in the name of the Corporation shall be signed by such officer or officers, agents or agents of the Corporation, and in such manner, as shall from time to time be determined by resolution of the Board of Trustees. In the absence of such determination by the Board of Trustees, such instruments may be signed by either the Secretary/Treasurer or the President of the Corporation in accordance with their duties outlined in these bylaws.

Section 4. Deposits.

All funds of the Corporation shall be deposited to the credit of the Corporation in such banks, trust companies or other depositories as the Board of Trustees may select in accordance with these bylaws.

Section 5. Gifts.

The President Senior Pastor may accept on behalf of the Corporation any contribution, gift, bequest or device for any purpose of the Corporation.

Section 6. Books and Records.

The Corporation shall keep correct and complete books and

records and shall also keep minutes of the proceedings of its members, Board of Trustees, committees having and exercising any of the authority of the Board of Trustees, and any other committee, and shall keep at the principal office a record giving the names and addresses of all Board members entitled to vote. Books and records of the Corporation may be inspected by any member for any proper purpose at any reasonable time as approved by a majority of the Trustees on a case-by-case basis.

ARTICLE TWELVE

Not in?

Church Ministry

Section 1. Minister Ordination and Licensing.

(Para. 1) Role of the Board of Elders

The Elders may ordain and/or license a person as a minister of the gospel after first examining the applicant's background, his moral and religious character, and previous Bible courses and/or independent study he has completed. Final determination shall be within the absolute discretion of the Board of Elders.

(Para. 2) Application Through Elders Board

Application for ordination and/or licensing as a minister of the gospel shall be on the form provided by the Elders. An application shall be either approved or denied within 30 days of the completion of the investigation of the applicant by the Board of Elders. Those applicants who are approved shall receive a certificate evidencing the approval.

(Para. 3) Ability to Limit Ministry Validation

The spiritual leadership of the church may at its own discretion limit any licensee or ordained minister to an area of special emphasis.

Section 2. Ministry Training.

The Senior Pastor and his staff may establish a School of Ministry, setting forth a prescribed curriculum and course of study leading to ordination and licensing of ministers. The School of Ministry shall prepare students in the knowledge of the Word of God and in ministering to people's needs through the gospel of Jesus Christ.

ARTICLE THIRTEEN

Church Discipline

Section 1. Disciplining Church Members.[31]

Only members are subject to church discipline.

Section 2. Disciplining the Pastor.[32]

(Para. 1) Criteria for Discipline

Should the Senior Pastor demonstrate immoral conduct, questionable financial practices or theological views that in the opinion of a majority of the Elders may require either personal correction or termination of his position, the Elders shall contact the Senior Pastor and then, if necessary, the Overseers for investigation and evaluation of any appropriate discipline (see Article 9, Para. 3).

(Para. 2) Process for Investigation

Should the Overseers be asked to investigate alleged pastoral misconduct, a consensus of three of the five Overseers is required to take disciplinary action. With such a consensus, the Overseers shall assume complete authority over the Senior Pastor; they may decide to remove him from his position or to discipline him in any way they deem necessary. The Overseers have no authority in New Life Church unless contacted by the Elders, and then only insofar as permitted under these bylaws.

(Para. 3) Motivation

It is the intention of the Corporation to protect the hearts of all involved in matters of pastoral discipline. With the method outlined above, the "sheep" never have to pass judgment upon their "shepherd."

31. This section provides for those occasions when the spiritual leadership of the Body needs to discipline a member of the Congregation. Because worship services are open to anyone, the opportunity for church discipline is limited to those who are members in accordance with Article Two. Thus, an immoral or dishonest member may be disciplined. There is a biblical requirement for this function, and it simply provides a legal limitation of who would be protected by practical church oversight.

32. The disciplinary procedures in this section can be applied in one of three situations:
   - *Questionable moral conduct* such as elicit sexual activities, etc.
   - *Questionable financial practices* such as stealing money, tax fraud or some type of intentional dishonest activity with church or personal funds, properties or assets, which also includes a flagrant lack of good judgment in personal business decisions and/or allowing business schemes to affect the church's fund-raising, causing harm to the spiritual life of the church.

• *Questionable theological views* the Pastor believes and teaches that are contrary to the theological views outlined in Article 3. This is to protect the church from heresy.

The Senior Pastor should never be disciplined for simple personal preferences. Decisions such as guest-speaker selection (unless the speaker is invited to teach a heresy with the support of the Senior Pastor), scheduling services, selection of carpet color or anything purely subjective are not the bases for pastoral discipline. Sound judgment is to be evaluated before he is given the position of Senior Pastor. Once in the office, the Senior Pastor can only be questioned and disciplined for a major mistake as outlined in Article 9. This guarantees him freedom to boldly lead the spiritual Body of believers.

This section also provides a benefit that is usually found only in denominational churches. It prevents the Congregation, Board or church members from having to judge or even talk about the discipline of their own Senior Pastor. Your bylaws or minutes of a board meeting should include a current list of five Overseers who know the church and the Senior Pastor. All five Overseers should currently be Pastors of local churches, and should be respected by your church and your Senior Pastor. These Overseers have full authority, once contacted by an Elder. Contacting the Overseers is the only way within the church to discipline a Senior Pastor.

ARTICLE FOURTEEN[33]

Amendment of Bylaws

These bylaws may be altered, amended or repealed, and new bylaws may be adopted, by a 5/7 vote of the Board of Trustees at any regular meeting of the Board, with the exception of Article 3, the Statement of Faith. Only the Senior Pastor with two-thirds of the serving Elders may change the Statement of Faith. At least five days written advance notice of said meeting shall be given to each member of the Board. In the written notice, proposed changes must be explained. These bylaws may also be altered, amended or repealed and new bylaws may be adopted by consent in writing signed by all of the Board of Trustees.

These bylaws were approved by the Board of Trustees of New Life Church on this 13th day of July, 1997.

New Life Church Board of Trustees:

33. This provision is for the amendment of the bylaws of the church, but only under extreme circumstances. Notice that written notice of such changes must be made five days in advance and that the majority (five to seven) of the Trustees must agree. This is the only time a quorum does not have the authority to take official action.

THE PHILOSOPHY OF NEW LIFE CHURCH

Many people credit the success of New Life Church to its philosophy of ministry. This philosophy includes six primary presuppositions for local church ministry:

1. Many people love God, but have become discouraged or disillusioned with "church." Therefore, a church that offers a personal encounter with Jesus and growth in His Word, without the clutter of an overly structured environment, has great appeal.

2. Many people love to give to God, but they resent the schemes that religious groups use to raise money. Therefore there are a great number of people willing to give if they are able to see honesty, integrity and genuine spiritual values reflected in the lifestyles of their church leaders. Every year, when New Life Church releases its cash flow statement, the church grows both in membership and giving because so many people respond to the respect given them (no pledge envelopes, full financial disclosure, reasonable pastoral salaries, etc.).

The giving of tithes and offerings is worship to Jesus Christ and is an expression of the relationship between the individual giver and the Lord. That is why we don't have people fill out pledge cards or make faith promises. Therefore, the government of New Life Church does not base expenditures on upward projections or pledges, but on the past history of contributions. Funds are not "income only," they are worship, and must not be considered as a business transaction, but as an expression of gratitude toward God. This has proven to be a great encourager for people to give financially.

3. Efficient church government. Many godly people have become disillusioned with church politics and church business meetings because they can readily see the carnality that arises in these settings. Therefore, New Life Church allows strong pastoral leadership in ministry matters, internal Board control (Trustees) in major financial matters, external Elder control for overseeing the Senior Pastor, and full Congregation rule in selection of a new Senior Pastor. Because of this balance, the believers are free to grow in faith and in relationships within the body, without the burden of an over-extensive church government.

4. Simplicity. We believe that the gospel message is simple enough to be grasped by all. Because of that, we keep our teaching, worship services and structures simple.

5. Jesus is the head of the church, and people are accountable to Him. Since the church is not Jesus, we try to communicate and emphasize the goodness of knowing Him, not necessarily the church as an institution. The church does not save, heal or restore people; God does. In response to that, we encourage people to know Christ and receive spiritual renewal. Therefore, we don't have formal membership. If God adds a person to New Life Church and they participate through attendance and giving, then they are a "member."

6. Freedom to choose. Because the Bible gives people the freedom to receive or reject Christ, the freedom to make decisions on their own and the freedom to

receive the consequences or benefits of those decisions, New Life Church also allows many freedoms. New Life Church allows people full participation in Communion, water baptism, all services, cell groups, missions, etc., according to the individual's decision. The church gives people freedom to develop many in-depth relationships or remain private. The church keeps individual giving records confidential, as they are seen as spiritual worship, not as a gauge of spirituality. The roles of the Pastor and church government are to encourage people to fulfill their calling in God through Bible teaching, counsel, prayer, discipline and administration. The roles of the Pastor and church government do not include excessive personal control or manipulation of people's lives.

This allows remarkable self-respect and personal responsibility in the lives of people. It is this factor that has contributed greatly to the growth of the church, because this allows people to feel respected, responsible and accepted. To the traditional church member, these presuppositions seem dangerous. However, these fundamental ideas have created some of the largest Protestant churches in the world. Most of the largest independent Protestant churches in America and throughout the world operate with most of these undergirding philosophies. And, consistently, these churches have grown as rapidly, and sometimes more rapidly, than New Life Church.

Put Your Prayer into Action

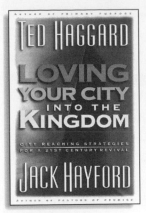

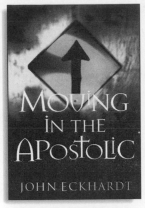

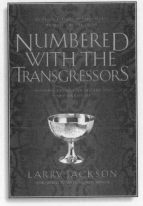

Loving Your City into the Kingdom
Ted Haggard & Jack Hayford
City-Reaching Strategies for a 21st-Century Revival

Paperback • ISBN 08307.18958
Video • UPC 607135.001119

Moving in the Apostolic
John Eckhardt
God's Plan for Leading His Church to the Final Victory

Paperback • ISBN 08307.23730

Numbered with the Transgressors
Larry Jackson
Changing the Way We See the Lost—and Ourselves

Paperback • ISBN 08307.21967

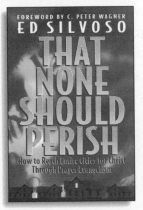

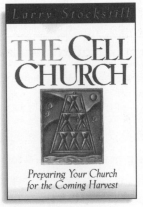

That None Should Perish
Ed Silvoso
How to Reach Entire Cities for Christ Through Prayer Evangelism

Paperback • ISBN 08307.16904
Video • UPC 607135.001102

The Cell Church
Larry Stockstill
A Model for Ministering to Every Member of the Body of Christ

Hardcover • ISBN 08307.20723

Healing America's Wounds
John Dawson
Hope at Last—an Amazing Report of God Breaking Through

Paperback • ISBN 08307.16939

Available at your local Christian bookstore.

GET LIFE!

Do you know emerging leaders who want to strengthen God's call on their life? **twentyfourseven** empowers young people through leadership training and great adventure all in the context of a healthy life-giving church. **twentyfourseven** isn't just another internship program—it's a calling to a whole new way of life. Contact the internship of New Life Church at:

web www.route247.com

email twentyfourseven@newlifechurch.org

toll free 1-866-247-1247

24 seven

WORLDWIDE

DEVELO(P)ASSION

LIFE-GIVING RESOURCES

CONFIDENT PARENTS, EXCEPTIONAL TEENS
Creating a Teen-friendly Family
by Ted Haggard & John Bolin

Ted Haggard and John Bolin give you an in-depth look at the five-step spiral of negativity that seeks to pull your teens into its vortex and offer straightforward interventions you can take to stop it. They help you vault over the communication wall between parents and teenagers. They reveal the importance of purpose and how to instill it in your kids. And they help you build the foundation of insight and faith you need to parent with confidence.
Available for $10

LOVING YOUR CITY INTO THE KINGDOM
Catch the Vision of Reaching Your City for Christ
by Ted Haggard & Jack Hayford

This resource guide is a must for your library. This book contains some of the best material from 23 of the most respected authorities on church growth, worldwide evangelism, prayer, spiritual mapping, church relationships, revival and city-reaching strategies.
Available for $10

LOVING YOUR CITY INTO THE KINGDOM VIDEO SEMINAR
Share the Vision of Reaching Your City for Christ
by Ted Haggard

Based on the books *Primary Purpose* and *Loving Your City into the Kingdom*, this video seminar outlines proven principles and lifestyle guidelines for uniting Christians in effective city-wide outreach to the lost. But most of all, this seminar will help you mobilize your congregation by revealing God's heart for reaching unbelievers. Show it in your Small Group meetings, Sunday School classes or to your congregation, and watch them be inspired to reach out in love!
2 video set - 200 minutes in approximately 1 1/2 hour teaching sessions. **$ 32**

FOUR COMPANION TAPE SERIES

PRAYER WALKING
Out Of The Basement And Into The Streets
2 tape series $10

FOCUS ON THE ABSOLUTES
Heaven & Hell Issues
2 tape series $10

LIVING IN THE TREE OF LIFE
The difference between the Tree of Life and Tree of Knowledge of Good and Evil. **2 tape series $10**

THE PHILIPPIANS 2 ATTITUDE
Serving Others
2 tape series $10

PRIMARY PURPOSE
Making It Hard for People to Go to Hell From Your City
by Ted Haggard

You can change your city's spiritual climate. *Primary Purpose* contains practical principles and inspirational insights on how believers can impact their communities for Christ.
Available for $10

To order these or receive a catalog of other materials by Pastor Ted Haggard
Call (719)-265-3109
Or order online at www.newlifechurch.org